Penguin Books

Quick, Answer Me
Before I Forget the Question

Lynette Padwa is the author of *Everything You Pretend to Know and Are Afraid Someone Will Ask* and *Say the Magic Words: How to Get What You Want from the People Who Have What You Need*. She lives in Los Angeles.

Quick, Answer Me
Before I Forget the Question

EVERYTHING YOU
NEED TO KNOW
ABOUT TURNING 50

Lynette Padwa

PENGUIN BOOKS

PENGUIN BOOKS
Published by the Penguin Group
Penguin Group (USA) Inc., 375 Hudson Street, New York, New York 10014, U.S.A.
Penguin Group (Canada), 90 Eglinton Avenue East, Suite 700, Toronto, Ontario,
Canada M4P 2Y3 (a division of Pearson Penguin Canada Inc.)
Penguin Books Ltd, 80 Strand, London WC2R 0RL, England
Penguin Ireland, 25 St Stephen's Green, Dublin 2, Ireland (a division of Penguin Books Ltd)
Penguin Group (Australia), 250 Camberwell Road, Camberwell, Victoria 3124, Australia
(a division of Pearson Australia Group Pty Ltd)
Penguin Books India Pvt Ltd, 11 Community Centre, Panchsheel Park, New Delhi–
110 017, India
Penguin Group (NZ), 67 Apollo Drive, Rosedale, North Shore 0632, New Zealand
(a division of Pearson New Zealand Ltd)
Penguin Books (South Africa) (Pty) Ltd, 24 Sturdee Avenue, Rosebank, Johannesburg 2196,
South Africa

Penguin Books Ltd, Registered Offices:
80 Strand, London WC2R 0RL, England

First published in Penguin Books 2007

10 9 8 7 6 5 4 3 2 1

LIBRARY OF CONGRESS CATALOGING IN PUBLICATION DATA
Padwa, Lynette.
Quick, answer me before I forget the question : everything you need to know about turning 50 /
Lynette Padwa.
p. cm
Includes index.
ISBN 978-0-14-3112889-1
1. Middle age. 2. Middle-aged persons. 3. Aging. I. Title.
HQ1059.4P33 2008
646.70084'4—dc22 2007025802

Printed in the United States of America
Set in Berkeley Book
Designed by Julie Schroeder

For Libby Padwa,
who makes it look easy

CONTENTS

ACKNOWLEDGMENTS

Many thanks to . . .

Lani Scheman, friend, writer, and quipster supreme, for her work on the Paperwork chapter;

Betsy Amster, my agent and friend, for her sage advice;

Karen Anderson, my editor at Penguin Books, for the talent and enthusiasm she brought to this project—and for thinking up the title;

Ed Fotheringham, for the perfect cover illustration of my generation.

INTRODUCTION

Remember the first time you found a gray hair in your eyebrow? Or cursed the type on a shampoo bottle? Or realized that the foxy guy taking your money at the campus parking lot could be your son? And that he probably wouldn't know what *foxy* meant?

No matter how hard you try to forget such moments, there is no denying that midlife will stalk you and ultimately overtake you. You can stuff your iPod with the latest tunes and stretch your thighs into the most extreme yoga postures, yet you will still end up facing the numbers 50, 55, and beyond. With middle age will come inexperience, as a whole new phase of life rolls up against your unwilling self. Your only defense? Knowledge. *Quick, Answer Me Before I Forget the Question* will soothe the anxieties that keep you awake at night, and amuse you along the way. You *are* awake at night, aren't you?

I was in my midforties when I first pondered the question that gave birth to this book: "What happens at the Hair Club for Men?" For me, the Hair Club symbolized everything that was mysterious and icky about middle age—costly, secretive maintenance routines and pitiful, doomed vanity. I was so curious that I finally visited the Hair Club headquarters in Los Angeles. I wangled my way into a meeting with a consultant by saying that I was researching the place on behalf of my boyfriend. The woman who met with me—her lush mahogany wig nearly engulfing her face—assumed that I was trying to force him into the club against his wishes because I had a problem with his receding hairline. She disapproved. I felt bad, but pressed on: Could she take me into a styling room and show me how the Hair Club worked? What was their special patented system? She refused and showed me the door instead. I couldn't learn their secrets unless I became a member. (I managed to find out anyway—see chapter 4.)

And that's sort of what middle age is like: a club you don't want to belong to, whose secrets both fascinate and repel you. This collection of facts, feedback, and anecdotal evidence is intended to shine a light on those secrets and give you a heads-up on what may be in store. The questions range from the quirky (Do taste buds age?) to the embarrassing (Is it safe to dye my pubic hair?) to the practical (What's a romantic way to suggest a prenup?) to the nosy (Do women like Viagra?) to the reassuring (Will I have to choose between Sin City and Sun City?). The goal is control over your future. If you know today that at 85 your most prized possession might be your teeth, you may be more inclined to keep your next dental appointment.

While delving into the odder aspects of middle age, I sometimes felt like Mr. Bill, the beleaguered Play-Doh character from *Saturday Night Live:* "There's plastic surgery for hands? Oh, noooooooo!" At other times I felt like Jack

Nicholson as the psycho author in *The Shining*. You may recall the look of horror on Shelley Duval's face when she sneaked a peek at Jack's manuscript and saw that it consisted of a single sentence written over and over. Well, this book could consist of just two horrifying words: Get exercise. There is no way around it. No matter what I researched—insomnia, memory, sex, weight, liposuction, digestion, mood—the bottom line was always the same. The more exercise you get, the better you will feel and the healthier you are likely to be.

So now I know what's waiting in the wings of my current existence. After hyperventilating for a few weeks, I realized that not *all* the scary possibilities would happen to me, at least not all at the same time. I am not likely to lose my memory *and* have to work until I'm 80 *and* care for an ailing spouse *and* become incontinent *and* shrink *and* lose my hearing *and* file for bankruptcy and then have to find a new mate. My research also led to some happy surprises. I found out, for example, that certain scents make you learn more quickly . . . that single men our age value kindness over looks . . . that Airstream campers are cooler than ever, and campgrounds now come with Internet access and tennis courts and clean bathrooms . . . and that there are thriving expatriate communities all over the world where midlifers live and play for much less than it costs here in the United States.

Best of all, I discovered that my peers, the baby boomers, are changing the options for our future. We have buying power and voting power, and if we want to get plastic surgery on our hands and believe that our biological age is 32, who's going to stop us? The way we travel, the medical care we select, the houses we build, and the communities we live in are evolving to meet our priorities. So even though I don't especially want to be 50, after writing this book I have come to the conclusion that there has never been a better time to do it. I hope you'll think so too.

Quick, Answer Me
Before I Forget the Question

one

MIND AND SENSES

HOW MUCH MEMORY LOSS IS NORMAL, AND HOW CAN I TELL IF I'M FORGETTING TOO MUCH?

"Worrying about memory can actually make memory performance worse," declare the experts at UCLA's Memory and Aging Research Center. Talk about too much information. That's the sort of Catch-22 that makes one want to bonk oneself on the head with a bat and be done with it.

Of the many concerns people have about growing older, memory loss consistently ranks at the top of the list. Some short-term memory loss is common among people over fifty, when the hippocampus—the part of the brain that enables you to create, store, and retrieve new information—begins to shrink. As you age, you process data more slowly, which results in the annoying but usually harmless memory lapses that afflict midlifers. Alzheimer's disease is the specter that looms over everyone who has forgotten his PIN once too often or blanked out on the name of a favorite college professor, but there is little cause for worry. Few people develop Alzheimer's in their forties or fifties, and those who do usually have a rare, inherited form of the disease.

So what type of memory loss is normal? It is normal for midlifers to forget new information, such as people's names, and to get that "tip of the tongue" feeling where you almost remember a name but can't quite do it. It's also normal to occasionally forget the date or to have mild difficulty with new tasks, such as learning to use a digital camera. You may have a harder time than you once did with spatial visualization—for instance, recalling faces you see infrequently or finding your way around a campus you occasionally visit. In general, it is normal for midlifers to experience a decline in motor speed, speed of information processing, short-term memory, and fluid intelligence (problem-solving).

The symptoms of normal memory loss—also called age-associated memory impairment (AAMI)—can be very similar to those of mild cognitive impairment (MCI), a more serious condition. You may have MCI if, in addition to the problems mentioned above, you have trouble recalling the names of objects, remembering the flow of a conversation, planning complex activities, or performing familiar tasks such as hobbies or balancing the checkbook. Right now there is no specific medication for MCI, but in the near future doctors may begin treating it with the same drugs that are currently being given to Alzheimer's patients to delay the breakdown of brain chemicals that deliver information to the hippocampus. Researchers are hoping that if these drugs are taken before MCI has progressed to Alzheimer's, they may be able to stave off the Alzheimer's altogether. For that reason, if you suspect that you may have MCI, screw up your courage and visit a doctor.

The symptoms of Alzheimer's differ sharply from those

of normal memory loss or MCI. People with Alzheimer's will not only forget a doctor's appointment, they will have no recollection of making the appointment even when reminded of it. They may repeat information without realizing it, frequently use incorrect or nonsense words in conversation, have difficulty comprehending complex sentences, and have an extremely hard time retrieving information.

If you notice a decline in your memory, take a brief inventory of conditions other than age that might be to blame. Sleeping pills, prescription and over-the-counter medications, alcohol use, depression, and undiagnosed atherosclerosis, ministrokes, or thyroid abnormalities may be causing your problems. Often the situation can be remedied either by ceasing medications or by getting a proper diagnosis and treating the physical disorder.

QUICK TEST FOR MEMORY LOSS

The doctors at UCLA's memory clinic use the following test to help identify subtle memory loss. Look at the list of words below for one minute. Then wait twenty minutes, and write down as many of the words as possible. If you can remember fewer than five, it may indicate a problem with delayed recall.

Dirt	Snake
Gallery	Lump
Lemon	Mantle
Vest	Elbow
Ambassador	Kettle

CAN DOING CROSSWORD PUZZLES PREVENT ALZHEIMER'S?

In recent years, much has been made of the "use it or lose it" theory of brain function. The excitement is based on studies that found that people with more years of education are less at risk for Alzheimer's than those with fewer years. If learning was the key, it seemed to follow that senior citizens should keep their brains busy with crossword puzzles, bridge, and other mind-challenging enterprises. However, a chicken-or-egg dilemma soon popped up. Did a better education make people more resistant to Alzheimer's, or were those born with higher intelligence, and thus more likely to attend college, naturally less at risk for the disease? A Scottish study published in 2000 seemed to point to the latter conclusion. The study followed participants from 1921 through 1994 and found that lack of mental ability in children was an accurate predictor of late-onset dementia.

Curious about the alleged links, Dr. Margaret Gatz, a mental health specialist at the University of Southern California, reviewed all the existing research on mental exercise and Alzheimer's risk. In a 2005 paper for *Public Library of Science Medicine,* she mused, "What could possibly be the problem with older adults spending their time doing crossword puzzles and anagrams, completing figural logic puzzles, or testing their reaction time on a computer? In certain respects, there is no problem. Patients will probably improve at the targeted skills and may feel good. . . . But can it hurt? Possibly." Gatz worried that if people are told they can prevent Alzheimer's by keeping mentally active, society might hold them personally responsible if they do develop the disease, the way smokers are held responsible for developing lung cancer. Worse, the Alzheimer's patients might blame themselves.

According to Gatz, there are three types of studies that have tried to establish a link between mental exercise and Alzheimer's risk. The first compares cross sections of the population. For instance, a study will compare Alzheimer's rates in people with college degrees to those without, or it will compare people who engage in leisure activities to those who don't. Gatz points out that "both education and leisure activities are imperfect measures of mental exercise," making it impossible to draw reliable conclusions from these studies.

The second type of study Gatz reviewed were trials that measured the effect of mental exercise on the cognitive function of older people. These trials tested traditional methods of memory improvement, such as writing lists, using a day planner, and practicing mnemonic techniques (like using an image to remember a name). The training increased the seniors' proficiency at specific tasks but had no effect on other areas of their everyday functioning. Since the studies are fairly recent, there is no way of knowing if the strategies reduced Alzheimer's risk.

Neurological studies are the third type Gatz reviewed. These studies, which are usually done on animals, scan brain activity before and after mental exercise. The studies show greater neural complexity afterwards. In humans, tests have shown changes in brain scans after memory training and after a two-week program that combined memory training with a special diet, physical exercise, and stress reduction. Those results, while interesting, are not proof that mental activity will affect the risk for Alzheimer's.

"So far, we have little evidence that mental practice will help prevent the development of dementia," Gatz concludes. While tantalizing, the findings all are susceptible to the chicken-or-egg problem: Are smarter people more drawn to mental challenges in the first place? Are their brains naturally more flexible and adept at solving puzzles or memorizing names? Would these same people be less likely to have Alzheimer's whether or not they blazed through the Sudoku each morning? For now, the jury is out.

 THE GOOD NEWS ─────────────────────

Exercise May Stomp Alzheimer's

The newest strategy in the battle against Alzheimer's disease has to do with physical, not mental, exercise. A number of studies support the theory that increased physical activity can reduce the risk of Alzheimer's, the most recent being a 2005 Swedish study of 1,449 people ages 65–79 who had their leisure activity monitored every five years since age 50. Results were exciting: People who engaged in strenuous exercise (that resulted in heavy breathing and/or sweating) for twenty minutes at least twice a week had a 60 percent lower chance of getting Alzheimer's than people who did not exercise. Their risk of getting any type of dementia was 52 percent lower. Results were even better for people who carry the APOE4 gene, a known risk factor for late-onset Alzheimer's. APOE4 carriers made up about a third of the study participants. Perhaps the best news is that the people in the study started exercising at midlife; you don't have to be a lifelong jock to feel good about these findings. Most of the participants walked or rode bikes to achieve their twenty-minute goals. The authors also concluded that exercising more than twenty minutes decreased the risk of dementia even further (the Alzheimer's rate reduction remained the same at 60 percent).

WHY CAN'T I SLEEP?

If you're sleeping with someone else, that might be the reason. One in four couples spend the night in separate rooms due to a partner's sleeping problems. Twelve percent sleep with their pets instead of their partner. On the bright side, midlifers actually get more and better sleep than younger people do. The National Sleep Foundation's exhaustive 2005 *Sleep in America* survey—the source of these statistics—found that 52 percent of people aged 50 to 64 are likely to report getting a good night's sleep, compared to only 38 percent of 18- to 29-year-olds. But that's little comfort when you're tossing and turning at 3:00 A.M.

Women's midlife sleep troubles are often related to night sweats and other symptoms of menopause, which we'll talk about on page 15. Otherwise, the standout causes for losing sleep are stress, your partner's snoring, and pain. Each of these may be exacerbated by the sleep-spoiling habits outlined in the "How Are You Sleeping?" quiz on page 10.

Most people who have trouble sleeping blame it on stress. Before you jump to that conclusion, think about how insomnia has affected you throughout your life. Do you rarely get a good night's sleep, even if things are going relatively well? If so, you may want to visit a doctor or therapist and ask about antianxiety medication. If your insomnia comes and goes depending on the level of tension and pressures in your life, it is more likely to be stress-related.

One quarter of the married (or partnered) respondents in the *Sleep in America* poll reported losing sleep because of their partner's snoring, jerking, or twitching. Snoring is by far the biggest offender, and the person doing the snoring is not usually the one losing sleep. As snoring can be very hard to treat, the sleepless victim often has no choice but to move to another room. Restless legs syndrome disturbs both the person twitching and the person getting jostled or kicked. There are drugs to treat it, but you might simply need to change your lifestyle (avoid the unholy trinity of caffeine, tobacco, and alcohol). Lack of sleep can seriously dampen the quality of your love life: Twenty-seven percent of partners in a sleep-deprived relationship reported that they had sex less often or had lost interest in sex because of being too sleepy. Thirty-eight percent said that the situation had caused problems in their overall relationship.

Pain is another sleep-wrecker, particularly as people get older. The first line of defense is to take an over-the-counter painkiller, such as Tylenol, Advil, or aspirin, right before bedtime (do not take extra-strength painkillers—the "extra" is caffeine). Painkillers with sleep aids, such as Tylenol PM, may help but can leave you groggy in the morning. Prescription painkillers such as morphine and codeine can fragment sleep and cause side effects, such as constipation. A new mattress, an exercise plan, and a visit to a pain specialist may be in order before resorting to heavy-duty pain relievers or prescription sleeping pills. Any persistent pain that wakes you two or three times a night is cause to see a doctor.

Over-the-counter sleeping aids, such as Nytol or Sominex, may be enough to solve your insomnia. Nearly all of them contain the same active ingredient: diphenhydramine, better known as Benadryl. A typical dose is 25 to 50 milligrams, and your drug store's generic diphenhydramine works just as well as the name-brand versions. (The active ingredient in Nytol Natural Source is valerian root extract, also available in generic form.) Diphenhydramine is safe for most people, but there are important exceptions, so read the label carefully.

The relentless parade of TV ads for prescription sleeping aids is proof that millions of us are awake at night. Unfortunately, many of these drugs have side effects that come to light only after they have been on the market for a few years—witness Ambien (visual hallucinations, short-term memory loss) and Lunesta (bad taste in mouth, dizziness). However, getting only three or four hours of sleep a night for months on end isn't healthy, and prescription sleep aids may provide desperately needed relief. A quick Web search of the various pills' side effects is advised before you visit the doctor, so you can discuss your options intelligently.

In addition to pain or a disruptive partner, the following personal habits might be undermining your sleep.

HOW ARE YOU SLEEPING?

Are you drinking more than three cups of coffee a day? Three cups contain 250 to 300 milligrams of caffeine, which is considered a moderate amount. Six cups or more is considered excessive.

Are you drinking coffee, tea, hot cocoa, or soft drinks or eating chocolate after 3:00 P.M.? If so, stop. They all have caffeine unless they say "caffeine-free" on the label. Diet cola has *more* caffeine than regular cola, unless it is caffeine-free. Decaf coffee has 5 milligrams per eight-ounce cup. Caffeine's effect on sleep varies according to the individual, but a surefire way to see whether it is keeping you awake is to have none after lunch or to quit altogether.

Are you taking extra-strength pain relievers? Caffeine is the secret weapon in over-the-counter extra-strength pain relievers. Each Extra Strength Excedrin tablet has 65 milligrams of caffeine, so if you take two, you're getting as much caffeine as in a big cup of coffee.

Are you drinking alcohol after dinner? Alcohol will disturb your sleep as much as coffee, if not more so. A drink or two at dinner is usually all right, but drinking right before bedtime to relax yourself will backfire. Alcohol dehydrates you, so after about three hours of sleep you'll wake up thirsty. It also causes fragmented, fitful sleep.

Are you drinking too many liquids before bedtime? The *Sleep in America* poll found that about one-third of people with insomnia woke often during the night. Many did so because they had to use the bathroom. Solve this by limiting your intake of liquids after 4:00 P.M., and especially after dinner.

Do you smoke? Nicotine stimulates your nervous system, just as caffeine does. Smoking before bedtime will make it harder to fall asleep.

Is the room too hot? For ideal sleep conditions, keep the temperature between sixty and sixty-five degrees. Fresh air is good, too, unless an open window will let in noise.

Is the room too noisy? If so, try earplugs or a white-noise machine.

Are you getting enough natural light? Some studies have found that people who spend a lot of time indoors, especially during the dark winter months, may suffer from insomnia due to light deprivation. Bright-light therapy helped them. Outdoor activity during daylight hours might work for you, and exercise is very helpful in promoting sleep (see "The Good News" on page 12).

Are you taking any other medications? Nasal decongestants, high-potency vitamins, steroids, and certain medications used for treating high blood pressure, depression, asthma, or thyroid conditions all may interfere with sleep. Ask your doctor to check on the drugs you're using.

THE GOOD NEWS ─────────────────

The Non-Drug Prescription for Sleep

Culled from the minds of America's sleep experts, here is a program that will help you sleep peacefully without drugs. It's a type of cognitive behavioral therapy, boosted by a daily dose of exercise. Before you begin, check the section above to make sure you're not sabotaging yourself. Then follow the steps below.

1. Determine how much sleep you actually need. Most people require seven to nine hours, but there is no correct number; it depends on the individual. If you only need six hours, it is pointless and anxiety-provoking to force yourself to stay in bed for seven.

You probably need more sleep than you are currently getting if you're irritable during the day, find it hard to concentrate, or have trouble staying alert during tedious situations (such as driving to work or sitting in meetings). If so, try adding to your allotment of sleep time in fifteen-minute increments until your level of alertness improves during the day. On the other hand, if you feel fine during the day but wake up every morning at 4:00 or 5:00 A.M., you may be forcing yourself to stay in bed longer than necessary.

2. Set your bedtime based on the number of hours of sleep you need and the time you must wake up in the morning. For instance, if you need seven hours and want to wake up at 6:30 A.M., go to bed at 11:00 to 11:15, allowing thirty minutes maximum to fall asleep and seven hours for slumber (it takes most people fifteen to thirty minutes to

fall asleep). This means that if you need nine hours of sleep, your bedtime will be 9:00; if you need six hours, it'll be midnight. Keep to this schedule every night, including weekends if possible.

3. Make your bedroom serene and welcoming, and do only fun things in it. People with chronic insomnia tend to approach the bedroom with dread, as it has been the scene of so much frustration. To counteract that psychological effect, reserve the bedroom for sleep, intimacy, and getting dressed. Make sure the room is dark, quiet, and cool. If a sound machine works better for you than silence (or a noisy house), use that.

4. Exercise, but do so no later than three hours before your bedtime. The earlier in the day, the better. Exercising too close to bedtime will keep you awake.

5. Allow yourself at least thirty minutes before bedtime to wind down mentally. Don't do mentally taxing activities, such as balancing the checkbook, and put away the work you brought home from the office.

6. Take a hot bath or shower before bed.

7. If you're in bed for twenty to thirty minutes and can't fall asleep, get up and do something relaxing and distracting, such as reading or watching television, until you feel sleepy. Try not to ruminate about your life, your future, or your job, since the mental activity will keep you awake. Besides, every problem seems dire after midnight, and the solutions you come up with at that hour usually look ludicrous in the morning.

8. Do not nap during the day.

9. Give the program time to work. In a clinical study of a similar program conducted in 2001, it took some participants as long as six weeks to see significant improvements. On the plus side, the improvements persisted when the group was checked six months later.

WHICH DRINKS AND FOODS HAVE THE MOST CAFFEINE?
Here is a handy list, compiled by the National Sleep Foundation.

8 oz cola	23 mg of caffeine
8 oz diet cola	31 mg
240 ml Red Bull	80 mg
8 oz coffee	110 mg
8 oz decaf coffee	5 mg
6 oz caffe latte	90 mg
6 oz cappuccino	90 mg
1 oz espresso	90 mg
1 oz decaf espresso	10 mg
8 oz instant coffee	90 mg
8 oz imported tea	60 mg
8 oz U.S. tea	40 mg
8 oz iced tea	60 mg
1 oz milk chocolate candy	6 mg
1 oz bittersweet (dark) chocolate candy	18 mg
8 oz cocoa beverage	6 mg

ODD ARCHIVES

Welcome to the Dreamwork Movement. Across the nation, growing numbers of Americans are keeping dream diaries, recording their visions on paper, tape, and computer disc. Many are joining dream-sharing groups. . . . Scores of devotees showed up in Arlington, Virginia, for the annual conference of the Association for the Study of Dreams. There they heard the latest scientific findings on dreams, traded visions at breakfast, and acted them out after dinner. The meeting's climax: a dream ball, with participants dressed as dream characters and symbols.

—*Time*, 1987

HOW DOES MENOPAUSE AFFECT SLEEP?

Night sweats are the biggest problem. Waking up several times a night to fling the covers off the bed or go stand in front of the open fridge is not very relaxing. As one sufferer recently observed, a fortune awaits the person who invents a blanket that will fling *itself* off the bed when your temperature starts to rise.

Night sweats (nighttime hot flashes) are caused by the hormonal fluctuations that accompany the early stages of menopause, also known as perimenopause. Specifically, the balance of estrogen to progesterone is out of whack. For years the standard cure was to put women on semisynthetic hormones, such as Premarin or Prempro, and instruct them to pop the pills for the rest of their lives. But when the 2002 Women's Health Initiative study announced that hormone replacement therapy (HRT) caused an increased risk of breast cancer, heart disease, blood clots, and stroke, many women stopped taking hormones and began looking for other solutions. Some gained relief from over-the-counter herbal products such as Remifemin (derived from black cohosh) and Promensil (extracted from red clover). Topical creams such as Pro-Gest (made with natural progesterone) may help as well. There are no long-term clinical studies on these products, but Pro-Gest has been on the market for more than thirty years, Remifemin for more than forty.

Other women are opting for bioidentical plant-derived (natural) hormones. The naturals have far fewer negative side effects (such as weight gain and bloating) than semi-synthetics like Premarin, but health experts warn that there is no reason to believe they do not carry the same long-term risks. (As of 2007, the FDA recommends that in treating menopausal symptoms such as hot flashes and vaginal atrophy, HRT should be used at the lowest doses for the shortest duration needed to achieve treatment goals.) If your symptoms are making you miserable, your doctor might suggest you try hormone replacement therapy for a few months to get some temporary relief. If so, natural hormones are worth considering. A good source of information is www .naturalwoman.org. The site provides a free database of more than two thousand knowledgeable doctors in the United States and Canada.

What about waking up at 4:00 A.M. cool as a Creamsicle but anxious as hell? Progesterone promotes sleep, so one theory is that when there is too little progesterone due to hormonal fluctuations, you feel more restless and are more apt to wake during the night even if you are not having night sweats. (If you suffered from nervousness and insomnia when you were menstruating, this may have been the reason. The body's progesterone level plunges during your period.) The products mentioned above may help with this condition too. If you'd prefer not to use them, the suggestions on pages 12–14 may be enough to see you through the transition from early menopause to the serene Catherine Deneuve stage.

Aside from night sweats and anxiety, there is little evidence that links menopause and insomnia. It once was assumed that menopausal women stayed awake fretting over their loss of femininity and the passing of their childbearing years. Current surveys largely rebut those assumptions. The good old midlife issues that haunt both men and women in the wee hours—children leaving home, parents becoming ill, career changes, financial upheavals, drastic reassessment of the meaning of life—may coincidentally occur while you are in menopause but are probably not triggered by it.

 ODD ARCHIVES

The unpalatable truth must be faced that all postmenopausal women are castrates. . . . Multiplied by millions, [she] is a focus of bitterness and discontent in the whole fabric of our civilization. . . . [With hormone medications,] breasts and genital organs will not shrivel. Such women will be much more pleasant to live with and will not become dull and un-attractive.

—*Feminine Forever,* by Robert Wilson, MD, 1966

DO CHANGING HORMONES AFFECT A WOMAN'S MOOD?

"I drive to work and look around the countryside and barely recognize things. Everything I do feels unreal and dream-like. I have to be very social when I get to work and that is a major energy drain on me. I don't want to laugh and talk; just want to sit at my desk and figure out how to get the hell through my day. . . . Someone please help me with similar stories. I feel so desperate." So writes suzyq2 on the "Am I Losing My Mind?" chat page of power-surge.com, a Web site devoted to menopause issues. Judging from the more than seven thousand entries on the topic, she is not alone. A sample of subject lines on the chat page tells the tale:

I'm riding the crazy train. . . . wanna hop on?
Doctor Jekyll and Mrs. Hyde

Treading water in a stormy ocean
Obsessive thoughts
Does anyone constantly wish they could run away?
Going crazy again
Brain fog worse—can hardly function
I am in hell :(

When it comes to a connection between menopause and mood swings, "some experts still dispute the claim," according to a comprehensive 2007 *Newsweek* article on The Change. The story, by the way, opens with a group photograph of ten midlife gals looking as giddy as a gang of schoolgirls at the ice-skating rink. *They* don't seem depressed. A few pages later, a group shot of ten middle-aged men has them slumped dejectedly, hands jammed in pockets, brows furrowed in anxiety—presumably about their dashed dreams and dwindling testosterone. It doesn't seem fair or particularly accurate.

The official line on menopause and mood, repeated in the *Newsweek* article, is, "Research proves that menopause doesn't cause a major mood problem in most midlife women. . . . In fact, here's a surprise: the majority of women between the ages of 45 and 55 describe these years as the best of their lives." That's good to know, for the majority. But even the optimistic writers at *Newsweek* admit that fluctuating hormones exact a heavy toll on the mental health of some women.

The mood changes of menopause are sometimes obscured or exacerbated by other stresses of midlife, such as helping elderly parents, getting divorced, losing a parent or spouse, or dealing with teenagers. However, certain symptoms are especially typical of menopausal mood swings. Some women suffer from depression; others from extreme irritability, like a triple dose of PMS; and still others endure the "brain fog" described by suzyq2. A change of appetite, sleeplessness, headaches, panic attacks, or a decline in your usual level of enthusiasm may also be the result of hormonal fluctuations.

All these conditions may be eased by medication, a temporary stint of hormone replacement therapy, or changes in your diet and caffeine consumption. Fortunately, bookstores and the Internet abound with helpful advice for women afflicted by menopausal mood swings. Be sure to run these suggestions by a doctor if they involve drugs or herbal supplements. Your gynecologist can be a valuable source of information, but some ob-gyns are more interested in delivering babies than dealing with menopause. If your concerns are not given serious attention, consider switching to a gynecologist who is more focused on the issues of midlife patients.

WHY DO I HAVE TO HOLD THE MENU FAR AWAY TO READ IT?

As we get older, the lenses of our eyes, which enable us to focus on items at different distances, become less flexible. As a result, we may lose our ability to focus on items that are close to us, hence the need for reading glasses and shampoo bottles with large type. Other common age-related eye problems include dryness and floaters, those maddening but usually harmless particles that parade across your field of vision (if you suddenly notice a lot of them, see an eye doctor). Night blindness occasionally becomes a problem, as the pupil becomes less adept at contracting and expanding in response to bright or dim lighting. One neat trick for people who need to use the bathroom at night and get blinded by the light: Use a red bulb. A red night-light won't keep you awake the way a white light can, and it doesn't produce nearly as much glare.

 ODD ARCHIVES

In line with a new concept developed by New Jersey ophthalmologist Neville Baron, pharmacists may one day be stocking their shelves with eye drops rather than sunglasses for the summer season. . . . According to Baron, a person could use the eye drops and at the same time wear sunglasses for cosmetic purposes. The eye drops could also protect the wearer from ultraviolet exposure from car headlights, fluorescent lights, and computer terminals.

—*Drug Topics,* 1989

WHY DO WOMEN SPRAY ON TOO MUCH SCENT AS THEY GET OLDER?

To be fair, it's not just older women who are guilty of this crime against fresh air. Teenage girls have been known to clear a few elevators too. However, older women are apt to overscent themselves without realizing it for a couple of reasons. First, our sense of smell begins to wane when we're in our fifties. Human beings' olfactory sense is at its most sensitive around age eight, and it plateaus from the teens through the forties or fifties. After that, the decline is fairly rapid. By our eighties, many of us will be able to smell only half as well as we did in our twenties.

In addition to our loss of smell, there is the strange phenomenon of odor fatigue. If you stare at a bright light, you don't stop seeing it after a minute or so, and if you hear a loud noise it doesn't get softer over time. Yet if you smell a strong odor, even a horrid one, the scent will seem to diminish after a few moments. That's because hearing and sight are triggered by waves of energy, whereas smell is triggered by mass—odors are carried by molecules. When molecules bearing a specific scent reach the nose, they latch on to receptor cells that send signals to a part of the brain that recognizes odors. The receptor cells must dispose of the molecules once the response has been triggered, and that takes time. If more molecules containing the same odor come along too quickly, there won't be any receptor cells available for them to latch on to, so the smell won't be perceived.

Older people recover from odor fatigue more slowly than young people do, so they stay immune to the scent longer. Your mom may be telling the truth when she insists that she must spray on clouds of cologne because it wears off so quickly. For her, it does. Perhaps it is time to give her a few pointers about applying scent.

You might begin by explaining how perfumes are created. All scents are made of the same basic ingredients: essential oils and denatured ethyl alcohol. A scent's intensity depends on the ratio of oil to alcohol. Perfume, the most intense, is made of 22 percent essential oils. Eau de parfum has between 15 and 22 percent; eau de toilette has 8 to 15 percent; and eau de cologne has only 4 percent essential oils. The most subtle scent is eau fraîche, with 1–3 percent essential oils.

Scents have different molecular weights as well—the top, middle, and base notes perfume ads refer to. Fruity, citrus notes are the lightest and are meant to diffuse the fastest; they are first scents you smell. Florals and spices are considered middle notes and stay on your skin longer than light notes. Woody, musky notes are heaviest and last the longest. Perfumes may take up to an hour to fully develop on your skin, which is why it's so important to test a scent in the store and wear it for a few hours before you buy it. Most scents will last on your skin a maximum of three hours, or perhaps a bit longer in warm, humid climates.

Where should you apply perfume? *Not* behind the ears or in your hair, because the oils on your scalp can distort the fragrance. Instead, dab it sparingly on other pulse points: the wrists, collarbone, ankles, and behind the knees. Don't rub your wrists together afterward, or it may "flatten" the scent. To make sure you're not overdoing it, you can simply spray some scent in the air and walk through it. In fact, the word *perfume* comes from the Latin *per fume,* which literally means "through smoke" and harks back to ancient times, when fragrant herbs and incense were first used during religious ceremonies.

As a general rule, other people should be able to smell your perfume only when they are standing very close to you. If they comment on it when they're more than two or three feet away, you may be using too much.

ODD ARCHIVES

The J.W. Toiletries, Ltd., division of Mem Co., Inc., will launch its third men's fragrance, Wall Street, in two Philadelphia stores this spring, to be followed by a national rollout in the fall. The fragrance [is] aimed at the man "who is longing to arrive or has arrived." . . . Display material and advertising copy describe Wall Street as "the fragrance of power," and the fragrance's packaging, in burgundy and brown with gold trim, is designed to convey a sense of prestige and material success.

—*Women's Wear Daily,* 1983

WHY DO AROMAS TRIGGER EMOTIONS?

More than any other sense, smell activates memories that are emotional. This is sometimes called the Proustian response, named after a famous passage in Marcel Proust's novel, *Swann's Way.* The narrator, Marcel, is absentmindedly dipping a madeleine cookie into a cup of tea. As he brings the madeleine to his lips, he is suddenly overcome by powerful memories of his childhood home. Marcel reflects, "When from a long-distant past nothing subsists, after the people are dead, after the things are broken and scattered . . . the smell and taste of things remain poised a long time, like souls, ready to remind us . . . and bear unfaltering, in the tiny and almost impalpable drop of their essence, the vast structure of recollection."

This poetic explanation actually offers a key to the science behind the phenomenon. The "almost impalpable drop" is a scent molecule, and the reason it carries such potent emotions is that the olfactory tract, which processes aroma in the brain, lies next to the amygdala, the source of emotion. They are located in the limbic system, the most ancient part of the brain and the seat of both memory and emotion. Memories triggered by scent are no more accurate than those triggered by sight or sound, but they feel more heady and immediate, more "real."

Most researchers agree that the powerful emotions triggered by aromas may be due to the role scent plays in survival: The first humans undoubtedly used scent to locate food and decide whether or not it was safe to eat. Other mammals rely on scent much more than sight or hearing, and perhaps humans once relied on scent more than they do today. It is not unusual for people to say that they can smell changes in the weather or fear in another person, and mothers can identify their babies by scent alone. It's easy to see how any of these would aid in the species' survival.

Aside from its memory-tweaking features, scent plays a crucial but seldom-acknowledged part in the emotional life of human beings. According to Rachel Herz, visiting assistant professor of psychology at Brown Medical School, people who lose their sense of smell due to an illness or accident report that their emotions are less intense and their experiences feel flatter. Without a sense of smell, food is often rendered tasteless. Taste buds only differentiate between sweet, sour, salty, and bitter—all the nuances of flavor are determined by scent. Given how much of our daily enjoyment centers around eating and sharing meals with other people, losing the ability to taste food is no small event.

Herz and other researchers have come to the conclusion that the emotion evoked by a specific smell usually depends on the situation in which a person first encounters the smell. In other words, our scent perception is more nurture than nature. If you once worked in a stressful job where the office smelled like pine room freshener, chances are you will feel stressed whenever you smell pine room freshener. Likewise, scents that might usually be thought of as noxious will activate positive feelings if they were first encountered during a happy time. For many Americans who have visited Europe, the smell of diesel fuel is a good example: It conjures up the streets of Paris or Rome rather than being perceived as stinking engine exhaust. As scientists continue to explore the olfactory system, we may discover whole new methods with which to alter our moods, our energy level, even our mental capabilities.

 EXPERT INPUT

Dr. Alan Hirsch, Scent Researcher

As founder and neurological director of the Smell and Taste Treatment and Research Foundation in Chicago, Dr. Alan Hirsch has conducted more than 180 studies on sensory phenomena and disorders. Many of these have explored how enhancing certain smells and tastes can affect eating patterns, mood, perception, and even learning speed. He is cur-

rently conducting studies on the effects of smell and taste on weight loss, sleep, consumer preferences, and sexual habits.

What should midlifers know about their sense of smell?
By the age of 40, people's olfactory ability starts dropping. That's important because it correlates with the age when people start to see an increase in weight. Part of the reason for this might be because the part of the brain that allows us to determine our degree of satiety, the hypothalamus, is regulated to a large degree by our sensory perception of the food we eat. If you can't smell it, you can't taste it, because about 90 percent of taste is really smell. You tend to eat more until you can get that sensory experience.

Explain your research concerning the way a specific scent can affect how others perceive our weight.
We found that if women wore a mixed-floral spicy aroma, sort of like Old Spice with floral shampoo, men perceived them to be approximately twelve pounds lighter than their actual weight. It's sort of like the effect of horizontal and vertical lines. If someone wears a shirt with up-and-down lines, they're perceived as thinner than they are. We found that the mixed-floral spicy aroma does the same thing.

Now, it did not work on all men. It didn't work on tailors. Also, here in Chicago there's a Six Flags where people guess your weight, and it didn't work on those men either. They're using other modalities to judge weight, a cognitive process like a height-waist ratio, whereas most men decide if a woman is attractive or not and then ascribe a weight to her.

How many different scents did you try?
Hundreds! It took us over a decade to do it. Originally we tried a whole bunch of food items, a bunch of perfumes; nothing was doing anything, and I was tearing my hair out. If doing as little as changing the pupil size in a photo causes people to perceive a woman as being more attractive, I couldn't believe that odor wouldn't have an effect. Finally, we found the mixed-floral spicy aroma that worked.

What other areas of your research apply to people in their forties and fifties?
We looked at the effect of odors on perception of age. We found that if women wore an aroma of grapefruit, men perceived them to be six years younger than they actually were. Pink grapefruit had the greatest effect, although I'm sure other things would work as well. Humans can detect about thirty thousand different smells, and obviously we couldn't test all of them.

What's your theory on why pink grapefruit worked?
One theory is that maybe the odor induced the men to be in a more positive mood state, and when they were in a positive mood they tended to view women in a more optimistic way. Possibly it has to do with sexual arousal in the male. When they're sexually aroused they tend to be more optimistic about how members of the opposite sex look.

Can scents affect learning speed?
Yes. We found that a mixed floral scent increased the speed of learning and memory by 17 percent compared to

a no-odor condition. We've tested it in normal kids and adults, and now we've begun to test children with ADHD to see if we can help treat that condition.

Is there anything else midlife men and women should watch out for when it comes to our sense of smell?
I think one of the important points is that you are what you smell. Throughout history, we tend to assume that if people smell bad, they *are* bad. In pre–World War II Germany, the Germans described Jews as having a garlic smell; in the United States, whites described blacks as having a specific odor; and in Japan today, they describe Westerners as smelling like rancid butter. You can use a smell to stereotype a group. For individuals, if you smell good, people perceive you as good, and if you smell bad, people perceive you as bad. If your ability to smell is diminished, you won't know if you smell good or bad, and you need to be aware of that.

DO TASTE BUDS AGE?

Not much. Adults have about 10,000 taste buds, children slightly more, including taste buds spread along the insides of the cheeks. Most people assume that taste buds are the bumps on your tongue, but they're not. The bumps are called *papillae*. Taste buds reside within the papillae, in bunches of 2 to 250. When we are children, our sense of taste, like just about everything else, is at its most acute. When we hit midlife, the number and mass of our taste buds diminishes, beginning at age 50 to 60 for men and 40 to 50 for women, but it does not usually affect our ability to detect sweet, sour, salty, or bitter flavors. What does happen is that our sense of smell declines with age, and smell determines much of what we perceive as flavor. For most people, this doesn't occur until after age 70. Researchers are investigating the possibility that decreased sense of smell and taste has nothing to do with age but instead is a result of smoking, disease, or environmental factors that have accrued over many years.

Scalding your tongue repeatedly can damage your taste buds, but eating spicy foods will not. That's because spicy foods stimulate the nerve fibers that are wrapped around the taste buds, but they do not affect the buds themselves. Spicy foods irritate your tongue and mouth; they cause pain, and some people like a little jolt of pain with their culinary pleasure. Researchers have yet to figure out why that is so, but one study suggested that the pain may trigger endorphins. Spicy food can temporarily dull your sense of taste, and the desensitization may last for hours. This in turn may suppress your appetite, making spicy food a good choice for people who want to lose a few pounds.

CAN I PREVENT HEARING LOSS?

Did you pack earplugs with your rolling papers before every concert? Did you turn down the stereo when Dad said to? If not, you may have missed your best chance to preserve your hearing. However, if you are currently exposed to loud noises, you should do all you can to protect what hearing you have left by wearing earplugs. A general rule is that if you have to shout in order for other people to hear you, the noise level may be damaging your ears. Noise-induced hearing loss, the only type that can be prevented, is permanent. Hearing aids can help, but they cannot repair the damage.

Music played too loudly—on a stereo, at a concert, or via iPods or MP3 players—is a major cause of hearing loss, both for teenagers and adults. The iPods and MP3s are especially insidious. Some can reach 105 decibels; for comparison, an aircraft taking off is 110. Other harmful noises include power tools such as chain saws, certain children's toys, farm machinery, snowmobiles, motorcycles, lawnmowers and leaf-blowers, firearms, and dentists' pneumatic drills. Keep in mind that it isn't just the loudness of a noise that hurts your ears, it's also the duration.

Regardless of whether or not you protect your ears from loud noises, there is still a chance that your hearing will diminish as you get older. Age-related hearing loss, called presbycusis, may begin around age 50, but in many cases it doesn't cause problems until later. By age 65, as many as 30 percent of adults are troubled by declining hearing; of those, 60 percent are men.

There is always the possibility that your bad hearing is caused by impacted earwax. The wax can be removed either at home using an earwax removal kit, which is sometimes sufficient, or in the doctor's office. If you go to a doctor, choose one who is experienced in this procedure. Inept earwax removal may result in permanent damage, such as tinnitus, a perpetual ringing in the ears.

WHAT'S THAT DIZZY FEELING, AND HOW CAN I MAKE IT GO AWAY?

It's called vertigo—that sick, room-spinning sensation that suddenly comes upon you when you look in the rearview mirror or get up from bed too quickly. Sometimes it goes away all by itself, sometimes it lasts for months. And sometimes people don't ask the doctor about it because they're afraid it might be caused by a brain tumor or stroke.

The truth is probably much more benign. In fact, its technical name is *benign paroxysmal positional vertigo* (BPPV). It can occur at any age but is most prevalent among people over 50. About half of all cases of dizziness in older people are caused by BPPV. The problem arises in the fluid of the three inner-ear canals, which are responsible for our sense of balance. Calcium carbonate crystals get dislodged and float around in the fluid, bumping against nerve endings and causing the dizziness. The crystals usually dissolve on their own or fall into the vestibule, a large chamber that connects all three canals. When that happens, the vertigo vanishes.

Occasionally, however, the crystals don't dissolve or fall away, and the situation continues to torment the patient. Happily, the solution is fast, simple, and doesn't require drugs. First, call an ear, nose, and throat specialist and describe the symptoms. Mention that you think it might be BPPV; some physicians are not familiar with it and many a sufferer has gone from doctor to doctor for months before being properly diagnosed. Ask if the physician knows how to perform the Epley or Semont maneuver (it may also be referred to as canalith repositioning). If the answer is yes, make an appointment.

At the doctor's office, you will be tested to make sure the problem is BPPV. Once the diagnosis is confirmed, the doctor will perform the maneuver, which consists of placing your head in a series of positions designed to shake the crystals out of their stuck location in the ear canal and move them back into the vestibule. A single treatment is successful about 75 percent of the time, but it's possible you will require a follow-up. You will also be given instructions on how to lie down and move around for several days following the treatment, to ensure that the crystals stay in the vestibule.

If you want instant relief, you can even perform a version of the procedure by yourself at home. It often takes several weeks to reap the full benefits, but you may see some improvement the first day or so. The do-it-yourself method is called Brandt-Daroff exercises. Search "Brandt Daroff" on the Web, and you will be directed to a number of sites that show exactly how to execute the positions.

If you are experiencing any loss of hearing along with dizziness, *go to the doctor immediately*. BPPV does not cause hearing loss, and this could signal a more serious condition. It's crucial to get treatment as soon as possible to avoid losing your hearing permanently. Also see a doctor right away if your dizziness is accompanied by one or more of the following symptoms: numbness or tingling; blurred vision; chest pain or changes in heart rate; fainting; difficulty speaking or walking; weakness in an arm or leg; or a headache that feels different or is unusually severe.

two

LOVE AND SEX

HOW MANY DATES DO I HAVE TO WAIT BEFORE WE HAVE SEX?

To the millions of Americans between 40 and 60 who are divorced, separated, or widowed, this is not a frivolous question. Plunged into the dating scene after being with the same partner for twenty years, many midlifers are baffled about the new rules for sex and dating. As a reference point, we have only ourselves. Were we dating in the freewheeling sixties? The instant-gratification seventies? Or the more careful eighties? Was anyone really that careful?

In theory, the sexual revolution that began in the sixties with the advent of birth-control pills slowed down considerably in the mid-eighties, as AIDS devastated the gay community and cast a cloud over sexual relations among everyone. But it's not so easy to turn back the clock if you grew up during an era when sexuality was celebrated openly and often. The Me Generation was not known for denying themselves pleasure, so it's hard to imagine many of them reverting to a prim routine of three-month trial-dating periods before ripping each other's clothes off. Are we still so impulsive?

AARP (formerly the American Association of Retired

Persons) was curious about the sexual attitudes of midlife baby boomers, so in 2003 they commissioned a study of 3,160 singles between the ages of 40 and 69, the majority of whom were divorced. What they discovered was "a vast chasm between men and women in their dating attitudes and sexual desire." Twenty percent of men thought sex was acceptable on the first date, compared to just 2 percent of women. For date number two, 12 percent of men would go for sex, compared to 2 percent of women. Date number three: 12 percent of men and a slightly more willing 4 percent of women. Attitudes appear to level out somewhat when the singles were given the option of "three or more dates". 20 percent of men and 18 percent of women found that acceptable. Yet the largest group of women—45 percent—maintained that they would only consider having sex after knowing someone for an "extended period of time." Five percent of the men and 15 percent of the women wanted to wait until marriage.

Bear in mind, the study reflects only what the singles *claim* is acceptable to them. It doesn't go to the next level and grill them about their actual behavior, but for someone who is reentering the dating scene, that may not matter. What's important is knowing how the other person is likely to react to your advances. Taking a longer view, the study also asked people what they liked least about being single. Twenty-four percent of men put "not being in a sexual relationship" at the top of the list, compared to just 12 percent of women. Among men, only one other category, "not having someone around" got more votes. Women placed far less value on being in a sexual relationship. In fact, more of them were worried about "nothing" than were worried about not having sex.

Of course, as Disraeli observed, there are lies, damned lies, and statistics. Make of these numbers what you will, men, but if you want to play it safe, wait until at least the third date to make any serious moves. Women who want to get fresh fast, go for it! You are much more likely to get a yes before date number three.

 ODD ARCHIVES ——————————————

"Prediction for the Eighties: Middle- and upper-class women—who are most responsive to feminism—will again begin to get married in their early-to-mid-twenties. They understand the good biological reasons for conceiving in one's twenties and are less concerned—thanks to feminism—about staying in or returning to the marketplace after the birth of a child."

—*Esquire,* February 1981

HOW MUCH SEX ARE OTHER PEOPLE HAVING?

Once a week. Yep, once a week. Despite the droughts that may occur after the birth of a child, despite the hints dropped by long-married couples ("Sex? What's that?"), sex surveys consistently report that most Americans are having sex an average of once a week. Maybe it's like believing in god. If you don't, you might not admit it to some researcher who's writing it down.

A closer look at the numbers is instructive. In 1972 a comprehensive, long-term sex survey was launched by the National Opinion Research Center (NORC). Every two years since then, the NORC team has reviewed detailed sex questionnaires from three thousand Americans. Since 1988, the responses have remained fairly constant: adults claim to have sex an average of 58 times a year. Breaking it down by decade, the study shows that the average for people 18 to 39 years old is 83 times a year, and that the frequency declines by about 20 percent each decade thereafter. Forty-year-olds report having sex an average of 63 times a year, which would put people in their fifties at around 51 times a year, or once a week.

The reason these figures might not jibe with your impression of reality can be found when the average is examined more closely. To reach an average, the total number of sexual encounters is divided by the total number of respondents in a particular group. But when the researchers tallied who was doing all the lovin', it turned out that slightly more than 40 percent of adults were having over 85 percent of the sex. A feisty 5 percent reported having sex at least three times a week. That leaves more than half of adults somewhere in the "a few times a month" or less category. Twenty percent of Americans, most of them widows and older women, have been celibate for more than a year.

As men and women age, it's natural for their level of desire to fade a bit and for the nature of their lovemaking to change. For some couples, it fades to nothing. Is that so bad? Yes, according to Walter E. Brackelmanns, MD, a clinical professor of psychiatry at the University of California, Los Angeles, who has been teaching couples therapy for thirty years. "Here's the problem," he told me. "Virtually every couple struggles around issues of closeness and intimacy. My interest in couples having sex in middle age, and even in old age (I think people should have sex until the day they die), is that it lends itself to developing a greater, closer, more intimate relationship. Now, some people say, 'My wife and I have sex once a month and we're happy with that.' I say, 'Great!' I'm talking about people whose sex lives diminish and diminish until they stop doing it. I'm currently seeing one middle-aged couple who haven't had sex in seven years. Having sex, by the way, is not like riding a bicycle. If you don't have sex for seven years, it's worse than the first time you had sex with that person. Much worse. You have to learn it all over again."

Brackelmanns's advice for middle-aged couples: "Don't settle for what you have." If your sex life has faded to a distant memory, it's worth the effort to see a counselor who can help you resurrect it.

 THE GOOD NEWS ———————————————

Quality Time

Even happily married couples are likely to have less sex as they get older, but apparently that doesn't bother them. A team of university researchers from the United States and

Norway found that men in their fifties are more sexually content than men in their thirties and forties, and just as happy as 20-year-olds. This was true even among those who had less sexual function than when they were younger. A different survey, by the Association of Reproductive Health Professionals, found contentment among both men and women at midlife: More than half were "more" or "equally" satisfied with their sex life compared to when they were younger.

For men, the reasons have to do with both physiology and attitude. According to the experts—psychologists, sex researchers, and health professionals men are often in their midforties before they can take their minds off the conquest and simply enjoy the experience. They're more patient, skilled, and often can last longer than younger men.

Women often approach 50 with fear and loathing, having heard that menopause will signal doom for their libido. Some do have to deal with a diminished sex drive, but many actually enjoy sex more than before. Despite the fact that their bodies aren't perfect, midlife women have a sexual self-awareness and confidence that is less common in younger women. Some even experience a rise in testosterone after menopause (testosterone is widely believed to control sexual desire in both men and women). Best of all, their now-patient hubbies or boyfriends are in finally in sync with them sexually.

I NO LONGER GET ROCK HARD FROM A MERE GLANCE AT A PHOTO OF A NIPPLE. WHY?

It's normal. In his book *Sex Over 40* (Tarcher, 1999), Dr. Saul Rosenthal explains that in your twenties, "just the thought of sex, seeing your undressed partner, or a fantasy about a sexual situation would cause your penis to spring to attention in a matter of seconds. This just isn't going to happen anymore. . . . You will require more and more direct physical stimulation to your penis in order to get an erection."

When Rosenthal, who runs the Sexual Therapy Clinic in San Antonio, Texas, first began treating couples for sexual dysfunction thirty years ago, "direct physical stimulation" was an issue, because at that time many women never touched their man's penis. In spite of the sexual revolution of the 1960s, there was still much prudery and awkwardness when it came to sex. A lot has changed since then, but certain fears and misconceptions continue to plague men in their forties and beyond. Rosenthal cites the following as the top complaints.

Not getting spontaneous erections. It's inevitable but should have no impact on your sex life, as long as your partner is willing to actually touch your penis, which would seem to be the least you can rightfully expect.

Not getting as hard as you used to. It's not inevitable, but likely, that someday your erections won't be as firm as they once were. Rosenthal says, "So what! As long as they're hard enough for enjoyable lovemaking, they can give you and your partner all the pleasure you want."

Not being able to maintain one nonstop erection throughout sex. This is not unusual but causes much anxiety among men. It can be "cured" by direct stimulation. Losing an erection only becomes a problem if it happens whenever you attempt to enter your partner—a situation that may be either physiological or brought on by panic and lack of confidence. Either way, Viagra or one of the other erectile dysfunction (ED) medications may help.

Not being able to ejaculate. It's normal for some men to find that they no longer climax every time they have sex. Again, the only problem with this is the anxiety it creates. If men try to force a climax by working harder and harder at it, they may simply lose their erection, leading them to feel humiliated and more anxious. Rosenthal advises men to relax and enjoy the sex whether or not they are able to climax. "If you're tired, under stress, or have had a climax fairly recently, you may not feel the need," he writes, Eventually, when your body is ready, you'll be able to climax again.

Not being as interested in sex. Like not being able to climax every time, the simple fact is that, as you get older, you probably won't be as interested in sex as you were in your twenties and thirties. You may not need it as often as you once did. You may have to be in the mood. The good part is, the woman in your life will probably be quite understanding about the "mood" thing.

HOW DO VIAGRA, CIALIS, AND LEVITRA WORK? AND WHAT ABOUT THOSE FOUR-HOUR ERECTIONS?

You have to love an industry that devises tools such as the RigiScan penile firmness evaluator and the International Index of Erectile Function. Both are used by researchers to measure the efficacy of the erectile dysfunction drugs Viagra, Cialis, and Levitra. In the United States alone, erectile dysfunction (ED) affects about one in nine males, most of them over forty. This translates into a market of about 30 million men eager to remedy the situation. Only about 10 percent of ED cases are psychological, which leaves 27 million men who may be helped by the medications. To understand how the drugs work, you need to understand erections.

When a man is sexually stimulated, his brain sends out nerve signals that cause nitrous oxide to be released into the blood of arteries in the penis. Nitrous oxide, in turn, causes the chemical cGMP to be produced. This chemical relaxes the smooth muscles in the arteries, allowing more blood to flow in, and at the same time compresses veins that carry blood away from the penis. More blood flows in, less flows out, the penis becomes engorged, and you've got yourself an erection.

The chemical reactions don't end there. The body also produces an enzyme, PDE-5, which deactivates cGMP so that the erection will eventually subside. As long as a man is sexually aroused and his brain is telling his nerve endings to produce nitrous oxide, additional cGMP is released to replace that which is broken down by PDE-5. The arteries in his penis stay engorged, and he stays erect. The cycle is broken at climax: No longer aroused, his brain stops signaling for nitrous oxide. PDE-5 breaks down the remaining cGMP, the arteries return to normal, the veins allow blood to flow out, and everyone either falls asleep or raids the fridge.

Sometimes, however, the balance of this chemical cycle is thrown off and the PDE-5 deactivates the cGMP before the penis has a chance to get hard, resulting in erectile dysfunction. Drug manufacturers reasoned that one solution to the dilemma would be a medication that temporarily inhibits the action of PDE-5. Viagra (sildenafil) was the first successful PDE-5 inhibitor to be developed. Levitra (vardenafil) and Cialis (tadalafil) are also PDE-5 inhibitors and behave essentially the same way Viagra does. In all three cases, a man who takes the drug will get an erection only when he is sexually aroused. The drugs don't cause erections, they simply allow erections to occur as they naturally should. The erections normally subside after intercourse.

Viagra must be taken sixty minutes before intercourse and works best on an empty stomach. Its effects can last up to four hours, which means you must be somewhat time-conscious in your seduction game plan. You're not supposed to take it more than once every twenty-four hours, so if you don't get lucky by hour three, you may start feeling like a teenager who has to get the job done before his girlfriend's parents come home. Viagra's possible side effects include bluish vision for several hours after taking the drug, headaches, upset stomach, and back pain.

Levitra allows you a slightly longer time frame: Most men will be able to achieve an erection twenty-five to sixty minutes after taking it, and it can stay effective for up to five hours. You can eat a light meal before ingesting

Levitra, but nothing too heavy or fatty, as it might delay the effects. Possible side effects include facial flushing and headaches.

Cialis offers the most room to move. Men can take it thirty minutes to twelve hours before sex, and it may be effective for as long as twenty-four hours. Cialis does not need to be taken on an empty stomach. Side effects may include headaches, upset stomach, muscle aches, and back pain.

What about those mysterious "erections of four hours or longer" mentioned on Cialis television ads? The voice-over urges men with these stubborn boners to rush to the nearest hospital emergency room—where the staff will do what, exactly?

The condition the ads are referring to is called priapism, and the chances of it occurring when taking Cialis are extremely low. Priapism is a prolonged, sometimes painful erection that is caused by blood flowing into the penis and being unable to flow out again. If you should be so unfortunate as to have an erection that does not subside after intercourse and continues for an hour or so *when you are no longer sexually aroused,* immediately go to the emergency room. It's crucial to treat the problem as quickly as possible, or your penis could end up being permanently scarred and unable to achieve erections, even with drugs.

Christopher Steidle, MD, author of *The Impotence Sourcebook,* cautions men with priapism to go to an emergency room where there is a urologist present, as "most non-urologists have little if any experience in treating priapism." Steidle treats cases lasting under four hours with decongestant medications, which decrease blood flow to the penis. If that doesn't work, he may use a shunt to drain the blood. The main point to remember is that the sooner you seek medical help, the more likely you and your penis are to survive the experience intact.

Viagra, Levitra, and Cialis each require a prescription and should be avoided by men who are taking nitrates, which are often prescribed to control chest pain. There are a number of other conditions that pose a danger to men considering PDE-5 inhibitors. Your doctor should be aware of these and screen you carefully before writing you a prescription.

DO WOMEN LIKE VIAGRA?

Overall, couples counselors agree that Viagra has been a very good thing for men with ED and the women who love them. Dr. Walter E. Brackelmanns, who advises couples on marriage and sexuality, explains the male point of view: "A man is a penis from the top of his head to the tip of his toes. If it doesn't work, he needs to go out and kill himself. If he doesn't get an erection or he doesn't have an orgasm, life is not worth living. If a woman doesn't have an orgasm, life goes on. She'll do it tomorrow. Women are much more interested in the sensuous and erotic aspects of sex. But if a man's equipment starts not to work, he can become very upset and unhappy about it. So Viagra, Levitra, and Cialis have been a wonderful thing."

Men have responded so ecstatically to ED drugs that the woman's perspective has been largely ignored. Most have been extremely happy with their man's renewed interest, but a few are less than thrilled. The changes in sexuality that come naturally with age, such as less focus on intercourse and more on tenderness, have felt comfortable to these women. Then, all of a sudden, they're regularly confronted with (as one therapist put it) "this big, hard penis." When a woman's level of sexual interest doesn't match her man's, he may turn to other women or to that reliable mistress, the Internet. The problem is rarely mentioned out loud, but it has been an issue since Viagra was first introduced in 1998.

According to several researchers who have surveyed couples using Viagra, the drug's price tag is partially to blame. Once a man has taken the costly pill, he wants to get his money's worth, regardless of whether his woman is in the mood. Dr. Annie Potts, a psychologist at the University of Canterbury in New Zealand, interviewed twenty-seven women and thirty-three men about their experiences with Viagra. Some of the women she spoke with reported that the price, along with the fact that it works for only a few hours, made their husbands behave as if they were entitled to have sex the moment the effects kicked in and for as long as they could sustain an erection. Niceties such as foreplay fell by the wayside. "You like to think it's an act of love, rather than just lust," one woman lamented. Cialis allows a couple more time to get on the same wavelength, which is essential if the sex is going to be good for both of them. "Viagra is not simply and only men's business," says Dr. Potts.

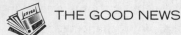 THE GOOD NEWS

Move It Out

Conventional wisdom has it that television in the bedroom is bad for sex, and in 2005 an Italian research team set out to investigate the theory. Sexologist Serenella Salomoni interviewed 523 Italian couples and found that those without a TV in the bedroom had sex twice as often as those with a telly. (The no-TV couples reported sex twice a week, while those with a TV had sex once a week.) Among couples over 50, the difference was even greater: Those without TV reported sex seven times a month, while those with TV had sex only once or twice.

SHOULD I USE BIRTH CONTROL IF I'M OVER 45?

The experts who offer contraceptive advice to women in their late forties have evidently never spoken to the experts who offer fertility advice to women the same age. Perimenopausal women in their midforties and older are routinely warned not to stop using contraception until they have not had a period for one full year—"You could still get pregnant!" Meanwhile, a 45-year-old woman who longs to conceive will be told that her chance of doing so without fertility drugs is only 5 percent, even if she tries valiantly for twelve months straight. Women older than 45 have an exceedingly low chance of becoming pregnant without using fertility drugs. If they do conceive, the odds are 53 percent that they will miscarry. (If you have already borne a child in your forties without using drugs, your chance of getting pregnant at 45 or older is slightly higher than the average woman's.) By the age of 50, a woman's chance of becoming pregnant is extremely remote.

Your birth-control decisions, then, will depend on your age, fertility history, tolerance for risk, and the amount of sex you're having. Some women find that even a 5 percent chance of getting pregnant is too stressful. Their doctor may advise them to take birth control pills, which for a long time were verboten for females over 35. Now they are supposedly safe for midlife women who do not smoke or have risk factors for cardiovascular disease. But birth control pills have some of the same health risks as hormone replacement therapy, so proceed with caution. Maybe the trusty condom is a better bet—they're much more effective now that you're not very fertile anyway.

WILL MENOPAUSE DESTROY MY LIBIDO?

It was once believed that menopause signaled the end of femininity, including sexual desire. The truth is rarely so clear-cut. However, the change may bring physical symptoms that can give some women trouble in bed, specifically, vaginal dryness and thinning of the vaginal walls. Both can cause sex to be painful and may lead to *vaginal atrophy,* a scary name that simply describes a shortening and narrowing of the vaginal cavity.

Vaginal dryness can be eased by using lubricating gels,

a transdermal natural progesterone cream, or suppositories containing natural estradiol or estriol. These treatments are a type of hormone-replacement therapy. Lifelong HRT has come under fire recently, but women with sexual problems should not automatically reject the use of all types of HRT if temporary treatment may dramatically improve their quality of life. With the help of an understanding doctor, you may find a solution that works for you.

What if your nether regions are technically fine but your head and heart just aren't into it? There is no denying that many midlife women do report a loss of sex drive after menopause. It has generated a lot of research, and the discussion usually revolves around a few issues that are interrelated. First, it is unclear how much of the decline in libido is due to the hormonal changes of menopause and how much is the cumulative effect of other factors, such as stress, exhaustion, and boredom with one's spouse. Researchers have found that some women welcome menopause as an excuse not to have sex with their partner anymore, because the sex has felt like a burden for a long time anyway.

Second, as with every other part of your body, your sex drive will naturally change as you get older. For both women and men, this usually means it will slow down. If you're comparing your libido to the way it was when you were 20 or 30, chances are you're going to feel inadequate. If you instead focus on how you're feeling right now, you might find that you are actually quite satisfied with your sex life, as the people did in the survey mentioned on page 39.

Third, there may be a physiological reason for your low sex drive that isn't related to menopause. For example, antidepressants such as Prozac, Zoloft, and other SSRI drugs are known to decrease libido in both men and women. Other possible culprits may be blood pressure medicine or antihistamines.

There is also the issue of body image—yours and your partner's. Much of the research on sexual dysfunction in midlife women focuses on how they feel about their bodies. With so much emphasis on youth and perfection in our culture, it's easy to feel unattractive even if you're 25. Aging only increases the anxiety. Intellectually, you may know that for every Teri Hatcher there are 10 million 45-year-olds who are not centerfold material, but the cellulite and saddlebags still make you feel like a loser. It's a problem even for women whose spouses crave and adore them.

So much attention is paid to women and their bodies that we tend to gloss over the other half of the equation: your partner's body. He is aging too, and sometimes no matter how much you love him, he simply does not turn you on the way he once did. It might not be right or noble, but as the psychologists like to say, there are no right or wrong feelings, there is only right or wrong behavior. In this case, the feeling has to be there in order to proceed with the behavior. It's a dilemma best solved by dual gym memberships and a marriage counselor who specializes in sexuality issues.

One thing all the experts agree on is that communication is key to a great sex life, no matter what your age. For couples who have been together a long time and become ossified in their habits, learning to talk to each other about what they want can open the door to whole new realms of unbuff but extremely satisfying sex.

Before we leave the topic of women's sex drive, it should be noted that there are some lucky females who actually become *more* sexual after menopause. Researchers credit the phenomenon to such changes as no worries about pregnancy, more privacy with the kids being gone, and more free time. They have also postulated that menopause may trigger a rise in testosterone in some women, and testosterone is widely believed to regulate female libido.

If testosterone is the answer, why can't women just take it like HRT? A testosterone patch, Intrinsa, has been prescribed off-label for women with sexual-desire problems, and trials showed that it resulted in about a 50 percent increase in desire. That sounds encouraging until you think about the wisdom of artificially boosting the testosterone level of a 55-year-old to that of a much younger woman. The FDA is not convinced such a usage is safe and has declined to approve it. Unlike hormone replacement therapy, testosterone therapy in women is relatively new, and there are no long-term studies of its effect on health, which makes it impossible to accurately assess the risk.

 EXPERT INPUT

Jeff Blume, Marriage Counselor

Licensed psychologist Jeff Blume has counseled families and couples for more than twenty years. He has a private practice in Beverly Hills, California.

What are some of the issues that send midlife couples to a marriage counselor?
In no particular order, there's money, there's the depression that can set in around midlife, there are issues about children, work, and the roles within the family. One of the main reasons couples come to see me is ambivalence. They aren't happy, and they don't really know why, and they're trying to decide if they should stay together or not.

How long have couples typically been married at that point?
About ten or fifteen years. That's when some of the issues that have never been dealt with start to come out. It takes a lot of work to keep the spark going in a relationship.

Is "spark" a euphemism for sex, or for everything—sex, excitement, interest?
What's happening in the relationship often happens in the bedroom. If people are bored together when they go out to dinner, and they're not really communicating, usually the sex isn't happening either. A lot of the couples who come in to see me haven't had sex for a year, two years, three years,

and now they finally want to talk about what's gone wrong. Why aren't they attracted to each other any more? These are brutally painful issues, and people really struggle with them. They don't want to break up the family, and some of them really care about each other, but they're not sure if they love each other.

Do you feel that their expectations for marriage are unrealistic?
Each case is unique, but typically what I see is that people have stopped communicating, or maybe they never knew how. They've been on cruise control and have not dealt with their feelings or resentments or unhappiness, and then it slaps them in the face when they hit midlife. Plus, the pressures in society now are just tremendous. The roles of women are constantly changing—they should work, they shouldn't work, all the different mixed messages. Problems arise when one partner, usually the man, is working all the time or is away a lot, and the wife is staying home taking care of the kids. She starts thinking, "What about my life? What's the meaning? I've been in the shadow of this man for all these years."

These sound like the same issues that have been around since our parents' generation. Has marriage really changed so little?
In some ways the issues are the same, and in some ways they're completely different. I've been in practice for more than twenty years, and one of the things that has changed

marriage most dramatically is the Internet. People have a new way to check out, emotionally—they just go onto the computer. Another big one, believe it or not, is the Black-Berry. One partner will say, "You're always on your Black-Berry! We're at dinner and you're checking your e-mail. Your cell phone is always ringing."

What advice do you give couples about this?
First I try to explore what's going on. Is it an avoidance of intimacy? Are they overwhelmed at work? Are they addicted to it? Of course they're going to have to limit it at some point, but I want to find out why they're using it so much.

What's also different from ten years ago is technology and kids. It used to just be TV; now it's the Internet and IM-ing, and parents have different ideas about it, so they fight about it. Then there's more pressure because they can't get their kids off the computer or the video games.

What about Internet pornography?
It's interesting: If a man or woman is having an affair, it's an affair. You know what it is. But let's say a wife finds out that her husband has been getting up at night when she's asleep, going downstairs, watching Internet porn, and then having a conversation with somebody. Is *that* an affair? It's much different than, for example, reading a *Playboy*. The Internet is far more addicting, available, and stimulating. And there's an interaction—you're talking to someone. You don't talk to your *Playboy*.

You could see a hundred million pornographic images online if you wanted to, and that is not an exaggeration. You could type in any category, and it's on your screen instantly. There are chat boards, message boards, the availability is right there. It often starts off innocently: "Oh, that looks curious," and it becomes addicting. Then the wife finds out, and all hell breaks loose. Sexual addictions involving the Internet are increasing at a rapid rate.

There's also the freedom of anonymity. You can say things you could never say to your wife.
With relationships in midlife, the communication has often gone sour, and there's a lot of resentment. Couples argue about who's spending too much money, who isn't giving the other person enough attention, who's doing more for the kids, who's working too much. Maybe they made an attempt to talk about these problems early in their marriage, but someone got mad, so they stopped talking about it and things got buried. The resentment builds. Then you go to the Internet and someone's saying, "Hey, you're so sexy and beautiful," and you think, "Wow, I never feel this way in my marriage."

What's really different now from twenty or thirty years ago is the availability of people to have affairs with. Back then, it was much harder for the average person to meet someone and establish a relationship. Today, anyone can walk over to the Internet and find whatever he or she wants in a couple of hours. I've been working with a man for six months who told me only yesterday that he's been having multiple sexual relationships with women he meets online. He's married. He has sex with the women at lunchtime. His wife has no idea; she's at work. Twenty years ago, would this guy have cheated anyway? Probably. But would he have had this kind of access, where he can just sit at his desk and, when he's bored or depressed or angry at his wife, go online and arrange to hook up with a stranger the next day? Not until now.

It seems like having children would be one thing that might prevent someone from going down that path.
The problem with people these days is that they don't know how to think. They react. They're just not thinking about the kids or the consequences.

Why did these troubled couples get married in the first place?
In psychology we call it the repetition compulsion. They repeat their past. People choose mates that are unconsciously familiar. The unconscious mind sets these things up or provokes the person to act out the conflict they had in their childhood. It's fascinating, and it happens all the time.

In midlife, people often come to therapy for the first time and realize, "Oh my god, I really did marry the wrong person." But they have children, or they don't want to make a change. From my perspective, midlife couples are the hardest couples to treat. Younger couples haven't built up the resentment; they're more workable. The older ones have already gotten through these issues. Midlife is a tough, tough time for a lot of couples.

Is there any type of person who is more likely to do well in couples therapy?

Yes. People who had secure attachments to their parents when they were children. Or, if they didn't have that attachment, people who have previously been in therapy and worked through some of their problems. It helps a lot if they have good communication skills. It helps if they really have love for the other person. And a big one is respect. We're finding out that this very basic level of liking and respecting the other person is even more important than communication.

Is there a message you'd like to get out to midlife couples?

When things start to feel bad in a marriage, get help sooner rather than later. Often when people come to me, it really is too late. Somebody is completely gone from the relationship. So when you first start to feel unhappy or ambivalent, find a therapist who is a good match for both of you and start talking.

WHAT DO MIDLIFE MEN WANT IN A WOMAN?

It would be nice if there were some specific data on this topic, seeing as there is a glut of research regarding the female traits that appeal to college-age men. Who hasn't heard about the genetic desirability of full lips and round eyes? Or the spellbinding charm of symmetrical features? Or the pull of the perfect waist-to-hip ratio? According to evolutionary psychologists, these physical traits, along with good muscle tone, clear skin, and shiny hair, are visual clues that a woman is healthy and fertile. From a purely evolutionary standpoint, childbearing is a female's primary contribution to humanity. Therefore, the more fertile she looks, the more males she will attract. This is called the good-gene hypothesis.

The same theory holds that, whatever their age, men prefer younger women because they look more fertile than older women. David M. Buss, author of *The Evolution of Desire: Strategies of Human Mating* (Basic Books, 1994), reports that the older the man, the more years he wants between himself and his mate. According to Buss, this holds true even when both parties are way past the age that any reasonable human being would want to become a parent. He found that men in their thirties are drawn to women five years younger, while those in their seventies long for ladies ten to twenty years younger. He also contends that the trophy wife is not just a perk who comes with success; she actually *increases* a man's status. One more reason to go for the younger gal.

There is no doubt that men are visual creatures. Given that midlife men are battling gravity and weight gain just as much as women are (not to mention hair loss), it hardly seems fair that they remain particular about looks into their fifties and beyond. However, the sex-and-relationship surveys also offer evidence that males are not quite as obsessed with large breasts and pouty lips as women may believe.

For example, men of all ages are less concerned with women's weight than women think they are. Twenty years ago, psychologist Paul Rozin conducted a survey of 475 college students. He found that "the female figure that women rate as most attractive to men is thinner than the figure preferred by men." Similar results have been affirmed in many surveys since then, but the one most relevant to midlifers may be a 2004 study of 172 married couples in their late thirties. Researchers found that most of these women felt that men favored a body type thinner than their own. "Even married women believe their husbands would prefer them to be thinner than their husbands would actually like them to be," write the researchers. "It appears that husbands tend to be more content with their wives' bodies than women are with their own bodies." Alas, many of the women were not even aware that their husbands were content.

One of the more interesting conclusions of this survey is that "husbands' perceptions of their wives' bodies may not be as strongly influenced [as their wives] by the current sociocultural ideal of thinness . . . although men may be apt to evaluate women's bodies when they initiate a romantic relationship, they may be less critical of their wives or women with whom they are in enduring, stable relationships. Issues of physical attractiveness, specifically body size and shape, may become less important in a relationship over time."

One of the few to survey midlife men about their preference in women is John Molloy, a marketing consultant and author of *Why Men Marry Some Women and Not Others* (Warner Books, 2003). Although the bulk of his book consists of snag-a-husband advice for young women, Molloy also devotes a chapter to midlife singles. He and his team of researchers spent six years, from 1994 to 2000, interviewing 2,543 women and their fiancés as they exited marriage-license bureaus. The men were separated from the women, and both were questioned about what attracted them to their future spouse.

Midlife men, Molloy discovered, are drawn to different traits than men in their twenties and thirties. When asked what first attracted them to their fiancées, the younger men cited personality over beauty. However, 56 percent of men over 40 said it was that the woman "took care of herself," meaning she was average weight, in good physical shape, wore tasteful makeup, dressed nicely, and styled her hair. The implications are clear: If a woman has "let herself go" (their phrase) at this point in her life, it doesn't bode well for the future. Molloy decrees, "While it is important for women to dress well and use makeup effectively when they are young, it's even more important after forty."

Although midlife men prefer women who take pride in their appearance, second on their list of must-have traits is kindness, according to Molloy. This is frequently mentioned by younger men as well, but for midlife singles the issue is pushed to the forefront because so many are divorced. The bitterness and mistrust that are often byproducts of divorce leave their mark on both sexes, sometimes causing women to become a wee bit sarcastic and skeptical about men. It is not a turn-on. If young men shy away from man-haters, midlifers are even more leery. Molloy dryly notes, "Mature men are often impressed when a woman is kind or considerate. Many have dated, lived with, or married women who were not kind or considerate, and experience has taught them that decency is more important than looks."

Molloy's research confirmed that midlife males like to date younger women. However, his study also showed that they rarely live happily ever after with the ingenues. The lifestyle differences are too jarring. Grown-up men don't really want to spend all night partying, and the girls don't want to deal with their partner's jealous fits whenever they chat with a man their own age. "Almost half of the men over forty who have dated, lived with, or married much younger women told us they would hesitate to do it again," Molloy reports, concluding, "Although men often date women much younger than they are, they usually marry someone closer to their own age."

AARP's 2003 survey, *Lifestyles, Dating and Romance: A Study of Midlife Singles,* bears out some of Molloy's research. The survey is especially fascinating in that it asks midlife singles what they look for both in a date and in a spouse. Men's top eight desirable traits for a date were:

1. Personality, sense of humor — 64%
2. Common interests — 44%
3. Physical attractiveness — 40%
4. Intelligence — 34%
5. Sexual compatibility — 31%
6. Moral/religious values — 20%
7. Someone younger — 9%
8. Sexual openness/willingness to try new things — 7%

When considering a serious relationship, the men are not as interested in looks. What's more important is sex. The top desirable traits in a spouse or partner:

1. Personality, sense of humor　　　　　　　　60%
2. Common interests　　　　　　　　　　　　46%
3. Sexual compatibility　　　　　　　　　　　37%
4. Intelligence　　　　　　　　　　　　　　34%
5. Physical attractiveness　　　　　　　　　　31%
6. Moral/religious values　　　　　　　　　　22%
7. Financial stability　　　　　　　　　　　　12%
8. Someone younger　　　　　　　　　　　　7%
9. Sexual openness/willingness to try new things　7%

It is food for thought, given that nearly half of the 57 million women in the United States age 45 and up are unmarried. Not all of them crave a mate, but those who do may have to abandon the much-beloved fantasy that has us all wearing muumuus and eating whatever we want. At least for a while.

 THE GOOD NEWS ────────────

Go Maybelline

In 2005, a study was conducted to test the good-gene hypothesis once and for all. Fifty-nine women were photographed and tested for estrogen levels. Those with higher levels (meaning they were more fertile) had more feminine features—smaller noses and chins, larger eyes, plumper lips and cheeks. Men identified these women as more attractive than women with lower estrogen levels and less feminine faces, confirming the theory. However, when the women wore makeup, the distinctions disappeared. Cosmetics successfully masked the effects of estrogen on facial structure, leveling the playing field.

WHAT DO MIDLIFE WOMEN WANT IN A MAN?

There is no lack of research about women and sex, women's taste in men, women's opinions of the ideal mate, earning power, muscle mass, ad infinitum. Indeed, it's a topic women can't seem to stop quizzing one another about. A visit to your local magazine stand will offer more on the subject than you need to read in a lifetime. Unfortunately, as with men, there isn't much research that relates specifically to midlife females. The 2003 AARP survey, *Lifestyles, Dating and Romance,* provides the most detailed look at boomer women's preferences. The top eight qualities these women look for in a date, from most important to least, are:

1. Personality, sense of humor   70%
2. Common interests   53%
3. Moral/religious values   39%
4. Intelligence   38%
5. Financial stability   23%
6. Sexual compatibility   15%

7. Physical attractiveness   14%
8. Someone to take care of me   4%

When looking for a spouse or partner, the women are a bit more concerned about financial stability and sex:

1. Personality, sense of humor   63%
2. Common interests   48%
3. Moral/religious values   38%
4. Financial stability   35%
5. Intelligence   34%
6. Sexual compatibility   20%
7. Someone to take care of me   11%
8. Physical attractiveness   10%

These numbers should put men at ease when it comes to the drooping and molting that afflicts us all. But no discussion of male sex appeal would be complete without a closer look at the things men *think* matter most to women. We're talking about the big four: hair, height, muscles, and penis size.

In chapter 4 we will delve into the topic of hair in great detail, but for now let's just say that it matters much less to women than it does to men. Most men experience at least some hair loss by midlife, so it eventually becomes almost a moot point. Women whose husbands have thinning hair don't particularly mind it, and those who are single and wish to ever have a relationship again are very tolerant of men's receding hairlines.

Height matters, but it's relative. In a 1993 *Psychology Today* survey about male appearance, most women agreed with the statement that being with a tall man made them feel more feminine. However, how tall a man must be depends on the woman's height and on how attractive she rates herself. Those who thought they were gorgeous were more insistent on taller men. Most women didn't want to date a man shorter than themselves, although one third would date someone their own height. In a 2004 study of more than a thousand women aged 21 to 54, the same sentiments held true. Women preferred to be shorter than their men, but as long as they weren't towering over them, they were comfortable.

The biggest gap in perception has to do with muscles. In all surveys, men overestimate women's regard for bulging biceps. Men love muscles; for the most part, women are indifferent to them. In 1993, only 20 percent of women found bodybuilders to be attractive. In a 2000 survey, 90 percent of women found them to be downright repulsive. In a survey from 2005, only 13 percent of women named a muscular build as attractive—and they were talking about moderately buff, not Mr. Universe. While women appreciate a man who gets some exercise, most care very little about deltoids and washboard abs.

Finally, the penis. Men realize that women don't care as much about its size as they imagine. However, it would not be accurate to breezily dismiss size altogether. You could tour the Web for months and not read every item related to this topic, but a *Psychology Today* survey provides a clearheaded perspective. The results, which are generally supported by online polls and chat rooms, show that width matters more than length. Women stated that a wide penis was "more satisfying during intercourse," while one that is too long can be painful.

Average penis length, by the way, is 5.9 inches. That number was determined by none other than Alfred Kinsey himself in the 1950s and confirmed by a 2001 survey conducted by Lifestyles Condom Company. The Lifestyles staff measured the penis length of college guys on spring break in Cancún, where erect penises are plentiful and eager for attention. Studies in Germany and Brazil reaffirmed the number. Average girth: 4.97 inches.

Men of all ages should take note of a factor that women in the *Psychology Today* survey went out of their way to mention. "We didn't think to formally inquire about such basics as soap, shampoo, and toothpaste," admitted the survey authors, "but the most frequently written comments— all from women—related to male hygiene." One women wrote, "What is the biggest turnoff? Poor grooming. A man who needs a shower, has dirty hands, wears soiled clothes, or needs to brush his teeth is a complete turnoff."

One recurring theme in the research could be called "Love the One You're With." Individual women seem quite content with the men they have and often deem their man's appearance to be close to ideal. Of women who wanted their men to lose weight, for example, most would be satisfied with a loss of six to fifteen pounds. Of women whose partners had lost some hair, only 18 percent reported being somewhat or very upset about it. Like the husbands who are happy with their wives' weight, women tend to adjust their criteria to suit the man they love. A 1999 AARP survey of midlifers and sex reported, "People find their partners more physically attractive over time. Six in 10 men aged 45–59 (59 percent) gave their partners the highest possible ratings for being 'physically attractive.'" Fifty-two percent of the women felt the same way. The only thing that sometimes seems to be missing is their telling each other about it.

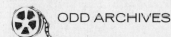 ODD ARCHIVES

From cities, suburbs and small towns alike, there is growing evidence that the national obsession with sex is subsiding.

—*Time*, 1984

WHICH SCENTS DO MEN AND WOMEN FIND MOST EROTIC?

Dr. Alan Hirsch, a scent researcher and author, has conducted hundreds of scent studies at his Smell and Taste Treatment and Research Foundation in Chicago. Judging by the research, he is particularly interested in how different scents affect men's perceptions of women (see chapter 1, "Mind and Senses"). To that end, he conducted a double-blind study to find out which scents get men most aroused.

INCREASE IN PENILE BLOOD FLOW PRODUCED BY TOP 10 ODORS IN 31 MALE VOLUNTEERS

Odor or Odor Combination	Average Increase
Lavender and pumpkin pie	40%
Doughnut and black licorice	31.5%
Pumpkin pie and doughnut	20%
Orange	19.5%
Lavender and doughnut	18%
Black licorice and cola	13%
Black licorice	13%
Doughnut and cola	12.5%
Lily of the valley	11%
Buttered popcorn	9%

© 2007, Dr. Alan Hirsch, The Smell & Taste Treatment and Research Foundation

Hirsch's team measured the blood flow to the penises of male participants, ages 18 to 64, as they inhaled various odors. The results are in the box above.

Of special note: Older men tend to like vanilla a lot, too (Hirsch doesn't say how old). So, girls, the next time you're in the mood for romance, bake a pumpkin pie, put some fresh lavender in a big vase, and maybe sprinkle some vanilla on the sheets. Home . . . warm pie . . . old-lady smell of lavender . . . erections . . . it's a little creepy, but the science backs it up. Actually, it sounds like advice for holding an open house.

Hirsch found that women also have some surprising preferences. They got most turned on by a combination of Good & Plenty candy and cucumber. The one scent that enchants both men and women is black licorice.

WHAT'S A ROMANTIC WAY TO SUGGEST A PRENUP?

The word *prenup* isn't romantic. It may never be. But the idea behind it is very romantic, if romance means love, trust, and belief in a future together. Whether you are divorced, widowed, or standing at the altar for the very first time, if you are marrying at midlife you would be wise to consider drafting a prenuptial agreement.

Second marriages, which make up the vast majority of midlife unions, have a 60 percent chance of ending in divorce. The best reason to write a prenup is that it can increase your odds of success. Once you have told your beloved not only what is in your heart but also what is in your bank account, it will bring you closer together. Hand in hand, you will confront the elephants in the room, namely assets, children, retirement, illness, and mortality.

Unlike twenty-somethings who blithely vow "till death do us part" without having a clue what that implies, you do have a clue. You can't be innocent twice. Still, you may feel you're being pessimistic or selfish for mentioning things like long-term care insurance and 401(k) distributions. It may seem the height of cynicism to celebrate your everlasting love with a legal document outlining what you will and won't commit to materially. However, ignoring the complicated realities won't make them disappear. They will merely fester and burble to the surface later, when you both might feel less loving and rational.

So how do you pop the prenup question in a romantic and reassuring way? The experts—family law attorneys—advise that the topic be mentioned lightheartedly as soon as you feel the relationship might become serious. If you can manage to trill, "Darling, I love you enough to sign your prenup!" as you clink your champagne glasses together on date six, more power to you. Or you might use current events to bring up the subject—there's always some celebrity who's talking about prenups.

Setting the stage is nice, but it is not essential. You can have a civilized and romantic prenup conversation any time that feels right. However, a calm and positive attitude is crucial. To achieve it, you might want to read a book about prenuptial agreements beforehand. *Prenups for Lovers,* by Arlene G. Dubin (Villard, 2001), and *Prenuptial Agreements: How to Write a Fair and Lasting Contract,* by Katherine E. Stoner and Shae Irving (Nolo, 2005), are two helpful guides. Either will provide valuable knowledge and additional reasons for requesting a prenup.

The first serious prenup conversation is best held in a public setting such as a restaurant or park. You could do it on a hike, in a favorite coffee shop, anywhere that is neutral. Because the word *prenup* is so loaded with negative connotations, don't use it when first broaching the subject. Dubin suggests that you begin the conversation by talking about a specific concern. The following icebreakers, excerpted from Dubin's *Prenups for Lovers,* are especially useful for midlifers:

- "Let's talk about our future, what we both want, our lifestyles, our present and future finances. I want to make sure that all our money issues are addressed and resolved up front. Then we won't have them hanging over us when we get married."
- "I was badly burned in my divorce. I would like to marry again, and I certainly don't expect to divorce again, but I have to be certain that I never go through an ugly scene like that again. I need to know what will happen in advance if we ever break up."
- "My children are very concerned about my marriage and what it might mean for their inheritance. I'm worried about this, too. Since most of my assets are from their father, they are entitled to those assets. They will be happier about this marriage if we do some estate planning. That will make me happier, too."
- "Darling, I'm worried about how my debts may affect your assets. I think it would be beneficial if we agreed to keep our property separate."
- "Honey, I love you, but what happens if one of us dies or we get divorced? Maybe we should at least discuss an agreement."

Your intended might very well breathe a sigh of relief when you say these words. On the other hand, your suggestion might be met with tears or a stony accusation: "You mean a prenup." In that case, you might say, "I hate that word, because it sounds so cold. I just feel that at this point in our lives, we need to be realistic about our resources and our obligations to our parents and children as well as each other. We don't have to decide everything tonight."

The first prenup conversation will certainly not be the last. But once the door is open, it can only lead to greater honesty and understanding. At worst, you will discover that the two of you aren't ready for the commitment of marriage. At best, you will deal with all the potentially divisive details before you plan the wedding, paving the way for a more blissful ever after.

three

THE BODY

WHEN IS THE BEST TIME TO HAVE A FACE-LIFT?

"Getting older is like going back to the earth," says a friend of mine. "Your color starts fading—your lips, your hair. You get drier. And things start to fall. It's all heading downward, back to the earth." Suzanne Somers would surely disagree. But is that our choice—Suzanne Somers or Georgia O'Keeffe? Not at all. There are many stops along the road to Abiquiu, according to the American Society for Aesthetic Plastic Surgery (ASAPS). Here is their suggested timeline for the cosmetic surgery procedures that are currently available. The ASAPS notes that "individuals age uniquely and at different rates depending on heredity, lifestyle, sun exposure and other factors," so the following is intended as a general guide only.

COSMETIC SURGERY TIMELINE

Identified Dissatisfaction	Cosmetic Procedure
—— Midtwenties to Midthirties ——	
Early frown lines between brows	Botox injections
Small or asymmetrical breasts	Implants
Localized fat deposits	Lipoplasty

Identified Dissatisfaction	Cosmetic Procedure
——— Midthirties to Midforties ———	
Gradual hooding of upper eyelids	Upper eyelid surgery or brow lift
Puffiness under eyes	Lower eyelid surgery
Fine wrinkling around eyes	Skin resurfacing and/or Botox
Frown lines between brows	Botox or endoscopic forehead surgery
Fine wrinkling around lips	Skin resurfacing/chemical peel
Nasolabial folds or creases	Soft tissue filler
Fat deposits in hips, thighs, abdomen	Lipoplasty
Muscle weakness/loose abdominal skin	Mini or full tummy tuck
Loss of volume/tone in breasts	Breast lift with or without implants
Spider veins	Sclerotherapy (vein injections)
——— Midforties to Midfifties ———	
Sagging eyebrows	Brow lift
Double chin	Lipoplasty
Vertical cordlike structures in neck	Neck lift/tightening procedure
Descent of cheek fat	Midface lift
Development of jowls	Lower-face lift
Slight drooping of nasal tip	Rhinoplasty
Thinning of lips	Lip augmentation
Pattern baldness	Hair restoration
——— Sixties and Beyond ———	
Facial wrinkles and creases	Skin resurfacing/Chemical peel/Botox/Soft tissue filler/Fat injections
Recurring facial laxity	Repeat face-lift
Excess fat and skin in upper arm	Upper-arm lift

WHAT ARE THE MOST POPULAR PLASTIC SURGERY PROCEDURES AMONG MIDLIFERS?

The ASAPS tallies the preferences of every age group. According to their research, the choices of 35- to 50-year-olds compared to those who are 51 to 64 reveal a practical bent in the older crowd. No longer so concerned with breast size, boomer women have turned their attention to eyelid surgery and face-lifts. (Females make up about 90 percent of the cosmetic surgery market.) Let's compare and contrast the five favorite procedures of both age groups:

AGE 35 TO 50

1. Liposuction
2. Breast augmentation
3. Tummy tuck
4. Cosmetic eye surgery
5. Nose reshaping

AGE 51 TO 65

1. Cosmetic eye surgery
2. Face-lift
3. Liposuction
4. Forehead lift
5. Tummy tuck

Some 50-plus women still choose to supersize their boobs and chisel their noses, but I like to think the numbers tell a tale of inner peace and self-acceptance among boomers. In 2005 (the most recent year for which the ASAPS provides stats), roughly 144,000 of the younger women got breast implants, compared to about 28,800 of the 50-to-65 age group. Younger women got more than 70,000 nose jobs, whereas only about 14,200 older gals did. Of course, it's quite possible that by the time one is 50 one has already done all the dickering around with structure that one is willing to do. At this point, it's all about what's draped over the structure—lifting, resurfacing, tucking, injecting, and lasering things off it.

Among the procedures most popular with People Like Us, what are the pitfalls? The industry has little data on this, but literature intended for cosmetic surgeons sheds some light on the expectations patients bring to the operating table and the disappointments that occasionally follow.

Cosmetic eye surgery (blepharoplasty). The goal for most midlifers who get cosmetic surgery is to look fresher, not freakish. But according to blepharoplasty specialist Dr. Frank Meronk, Jr., patients who are unsatisfied with the results of a technically successful eye procedure usually *did* expect to look "different" rather than refreshed, whether or not they admitted it to themselves or the doctor. They may have wanted their eyelids to look like another person's (usually a celebrity); they may have requested a very conservative eye lift and were then disappointed that it didn't look different enough; or they may have "harbored unrealistic expectations about precision." Other patients underestimated the discomfort and time it took to fully recover.

On his Web site, Dr. Meronk offers this reminder to eye surgeons and their patients: *"The delicate tissues of the eyelid are notoriously unforgiving* [his emphasis] in their response to overzealous surgery and even more unforgiving to attempts to undo the damage. . . . While many flaws may resolve or be blunted with time (3–6 months or more), more resistant difficulties may sometimes require further surgery. Seeking additional surgery to 'perfect' an already acceptable result, however, is rarely advisable and may result in unexpected outcomes. Unrealistic expectations are seldom remedied by revisional surgery."

Having said all that, are blepharoplasty patients usually satisfied? An extensive search for objective studies on the topic turned up nothing, but the fact that so many people continue to have the procedure points to the likelihood that many are happy with the results.

Face-lifts and forehead lifts. The amusing Dr. Meronk, quoted above, has this advice for people who wish to avoid sagging facial skin:

- Don't smoke.
- Don't rub your eyelids constantly.
- Be extremely selective when picking out your parents.
- Die in your early thirties.

For everyone else, there are face-lifts. We have all seen what can go wrong with them. How can you be sure you won't end up looking like Nefertiti? It's all about realistic expectations and communicating honestly with a skilled, very experienced plastic surgeon. While face and brow lifts can tighten the skin, they cannot change the texture of it. "Facial skin conditions such as fine lines, acne scars, age spots and smoker's creases will quickly return to their original texture and presentation regardless of how tightly the skin is pulled during a facelift," say the doctors at cosmeticsurgery.com. "Skin treatments such as laser resurfacing and chemical peels may be used in conjunction with a facelift in an effort to improve the texture of the skin and minimize the appearance of wrinkles, age spots, etc." Results can vary dramatically from person to person. The best candidates for face-lifts are people with a strong, well-defined bone structure whose skin has begun to sag but still retains good elasticity.

Liposuction. According to Dr. Patrick Hudson, who practices cosmetic surgery in Albuquerque, New Mexico, patient satisfaction with liposuction has a lot to do with which part of the body is treated. Complications are less common and satisfaction greatest when it is performed on the abdomen, outer thigh, calf, and knees. The areas that patients are less likely to be satisfied with include the buttocks, inner thigh, and suction of the breast in men. Some patients are reportedly unhappy with surface irregularity or because the doctor took out too much or too little fat.

Tummy tuck (abdominoplasty). If your abdomen needs more than fat removal, you can opt for a tummy tuck instead of liposuction. The procedure is more difficult and requires a longer recovery period, but it can correct more severe problems. The tummy tuck can accomplish near miracles in terms of removing excess skin and tightening the inner girdle of cartilage, called the fascia, that supports the abdomen. Tummy tucks can also remove fat and stretch marks in the lower abdomen (but not the upper). The downside is that a tummy tuck is more painful, requires a longer recovery period, and will leave a scar that can run as long as two feet across the entire width of your lower abdomen. (The scars don't show in a one-piece bathing suit.) In the course of the operation your belly button may be relocated as well, resulting in a circular scar around it.

After liposuction, the skin shrinks, just as it does after pregnancy, so most people do not need a tummy tuck to deal with excess skin. In many instances, it is too dangerous to do both at the same time. Tummy tucks are for more extreme cases; for example, people who have lost a lot of weight and are left with masses of extra skin, or women whose abdomens stretched a great deal during pregnancy. After the operation, your abdomen may feel numb for six months or longer. The final result won't be evident until the scar has matured, in about one year. Some scars fade, but others remain quite visible indefinitely. There is no denying that the tummy tuck can be an arduous surgery, but it also can dramatically improve your appearance and self-esteem.

WHAT HAPPENS TO THE SPOT WHERE I HAD LIPOSUCTION WHEN THE FAT COMES BACK?

Maybe it won't come back. That's always a possibility. According to one of the few surveys on the topic, conducted in 2003 by Ron Rohrich, MD, 57 percent of people who have liposuction either lose weight or experience no weight change after the procedure. The remaining 43 percent do gain weight, and for them the burning question is how, when, and where the fat will reappear. Much of the confusion is due to misunderstandings about whether fat cells can "come back," stretch, or spring anew in areas that have been suctioned.

The fat cells that have been removed via liposuction can never come back, and as long as you gain no more than ten pounds after the operation, it's unlikely that fat will return to the area that has been treated. Instead, other areas will gain more than they used to. The weight has to go *somewhere*. If you gain a significant amount—some experts put the figure at 10 percent or more of your body weight—connective tissue cells may morph into brand-new fat cells, even in areas that were liposuctioned. Before that happens, the existing fat cells will expand to accumulate extra fat (there are always some fat cells left in the area that has been suctioned). However, even if new fat cells develop in the treated area, there will still be fewer than before, and most of the additional weight will go to untreated areas.

The key to staving off weight gain after liposuction is diet and exercise. "Liposuction is not a weight loss tool!" warns every clinic, Web site, and brochure attempting to sell the procedure. It's a means of body sculpting—removing pockets of fat that can't be controlled by the usual methods. Of the patients Rohrich surveyed, those who exercised and adhered to a healthy diet were twice as likely to lose additional weight as their less-active, Frito-munching counterparts. The couch potatoes were ten times more likely to be dissatisfied with their liposuction results.

The most weight a liposuction treatment can safely eliminate during a single session is six to eight pounds. Beyond that, the patient has to have additional surgeries. Liposuction is a real operation with all the risk that entails, and the more sessions you undergo, the higher your risk of complications.

IS THERE PLASTIC SURGERY FOR HANDS?

Until very recently, hands were the dead giveaway of age. Even if you face-lifted yourself into the realm of the eerily ageless, your veiny, bony, spotty hands would reveal the truth as surely as Dorian Gray's portrait. And unlike your face, which requires a mirror for personal viewing, hands are impossible to ignore.

Traditionally the only option for treating old-looking hands was to bleach the age spots with hydroquinone, a technique that only works on fair-skinned people and sometimes causes irritation. Today, cosmetic surgeons and dermatologists offer more sophisticated solutions.

Age spots can be treated by any method that destroys the uppermost layer of the skin, such as sanding, freezing, or chemical peels. However, because those techniques may leave scarring, the current method of choice is laser. Laser treatment is also less painful, more precise, and requires less healing time. For many people, Retin-A and bleaching creams do a good enough job. Age spots are caused by sun exposure, so if you don't currently have any spots, you can avoid them by diligently using hand cream that contains sunscreen. The creams are available in SPFs of 4 to 30; most are 10 or 15. Golfers or people who spend a lot of time in the car, with their hands on the steering wheel, may opt for the higher SPFs or sun-protective gloves.

Bony hands can be plumped with injections of fat, but it is a painful procedure that leaves scars on your wrists reminiscent of a suicide attempt. The injections also may cause your hands to be discolored for months. To make matters worse, the fat is sometimes absorbed back into the body, leaving the hands bony again. Currently fashionable among wealthy ladies on the east and west coasts—and not fully embraced even by them—the procedure needs much improvement before gaining widespread acceptance.

Ropy veins can be eliminated by removing the veins, a scary-sounding procedure that is actually quite safe. It is called sclerotherapy and is the same technique used to treat varicose veins. Sclerotherapy involves injecting a substance into the vein that causes it to collapse. Eventually, the collapsed vein is reabsorbed into the body. The procedure is relatively painless, but there may be mild swelling and tenderness for a few days after treatment.

WHAT'S THE DIFFERENCE BETWEEN RETINOIDS, ALPHA-HYDROXY ACIDS, AND ANTIOXIDANTS?

Retinoids, such as Retin-A (tretinoin), are vitamin A derivatives. Retin-A is the only topical cream that has been proven to decrease wrinkles. Clinical studies show that it can smooth fine lines, reduce age spots, improve surface texture, decrease the size of pores, and give the skin a rosy glow. It has only a minor effect on deep wrinkles, such as laugh lines or the lines between your brows. Retin-A works its magic by increasing collagen synthesis and epidermal thickness.

The effects of Retin-A take between two and six months to become noticeable. During the first few weeks of use, most users experience itching, dryness, redness, burning, or peeling. It usually clears up, but some people continue to have problems and must stop using the product. Another drawback to Retin-A is that, even after the itching and peeling stops, your skin remains sensitive to sunlight and burns more easily than before. Wearing sunscreen is essential, and Retin-A users are advised to stay out of strong sunlight during the hottest part of the day. The cream is available in prescription form, sold as Retin-A, Renova, or Avita.

Retin-A is not your only choice of vitamin A treatment. There is also **retinol**, a natural form of vitamin A that until recently could not be stabilized in a cream form because it was easily broken down by ultraviolet radiation. Manufacturers claim to have solved that problem, selling retinol creams over the counter in UV-protected containers. Some early studies show that retinol causes fewer side effects than Retin-A and may be as effective if used in the right concentrations. Unfortunately, retinol creams are not regulated by the FDA, so you can never be sure how much retinol you are getting in a given product.

Word of warning: All vitamin A derivatives can cause birth defects. They should not be used by women who are pregnant or may become pregnant.

Alpha-hydroxy acids (AHAs) exfoliate the top layer of skin cells, thus encouraging new skin to grow. They may stimulate elastin and collagen production as well. Most over-the-counter AHA creams contain glycolic acid, usually in concentrations of 2 percent to 10 percent, and you apply them daily or every other day. Prescription-strength creams are available in 12 percent or more, and chemical peels administered by a doctor are at the 30 to 70 level. You can get 60 percent–concentration AHA peels over the Internet without a prescription, but it's not advised. Side effects can include itching, burning, and occasionally scarring. The stronger the dose, the greater your risk of side effects, but the sensitivity of people's skin varies widely, and many women have no problems with the over-the-counter creams. As with Retin-A and retinol, people who use AHAs should wear sunscreen and stay out of intense sunlight. *Consumer Reports* notes that even in the strongest concentrations, "no reliable studies have shown that these peels are consistently effective."

Antioxidants. The theory behind antioxidants is that they prevent damage to the skin caused by free radicals. Free radicals are unstable atoms or groups of atoms that attempt to stabilize themselves by snatching an electron from a nearby molecule. That molecule is then destabilized, and must rob an electron from another molecule, starting a chain reaction. The process damages cells, including epidermal cells. Antioxidants may protect against free radical damage by stopping the chain reaction. Exposure to sunlight reduces antioxidants in the skin, and antioxidant face creams aim to replace them. The creams also may reduce wrinkles and thicken the skin.

In the past, there have been problems with delivering the

antioxidant (usually ascorbic acid, or vitamin C) because it is unstable itself. Those problems have supposedly been ironed out by newer creams, but they are not regulated, and there is no way of telling how much antioxidant is actually contained in each product.

IF I STOP SMOKING, WILL MY SMOKING-RELATED WRINKLES FADE?

Although aging and exposure to sunlight contribute to wrinkles, smoking greatly exacerbates the process. Nicotine constricts blood vessels in the skin's outermost layers, restricting blood flow and starving the skin of nutrients and oxygen. Smoking upsets the cellular balance in the skin, causing collagen to degrade, which leads to premature wrinkles. One study published in *The Lancet* in 2001 revealed this effect in the skin of the *buttocks* of volunteers, suggesting that smoking causes collagen loss even in skin that never sees the light of day. The squinting and lip-pursing one does while smoking causes additional crow's-feet and wrinkles around the lips. Women are more susceptible to smoke-related damage than men because their skin tone is more delicate, but both sexes will suffer premature wrinkles and sagging if they smoke. Changes in skin tone have been seen in people who have smoked for as little as ten years.

Unfortunately, the wrinkles caused by smoking are not reversible. However, the moment you quit, you protect your skin from any further damage, and your skin tone will probably improve as well.

ODD ARCHIVES ————————————————

If excessive smoking actually plays a role in the production
of lung cancer, it seems to be a minor one.
              —Dr. W. C. Heuper, National Cancer Institute, 1954.

IS IT TOO LATE TO START FLOSSING?

A friend of mine once recounted the years she spent working
as a college intern in an assisted-living home. She had lots of
fascinating stories from the far-off land of old age, but I only
remember one. When I asked her, "What matters most to
these people?" she instantly responded, "Their teeth." The way
she told it, the single pleasure left in their lives was eating, and
if they didn't have good teeth, it was a source of constant complaint and aggravation. The image of gaunt 90-year-olds an-
grily gumming Wonder Bread has haunted me ever since.

As it turns out, the consequences of poor dental hygiene
are even more serious than I imagined. Periodontal disease affects millions of people, and the ramifications go way beyond
simply looking like a hillbilly if you lose a few teeth. Gum
disease has been linked to kidney disease, diabetes, and cardiovascular disease. The body is not meant to filter a contin-
uous stream of bacteria, which is what it is forced to do when
periodontal disease creates pockets of infection at the roots of
teeth. The inflammation in the mouth leads to inflammation
elsewhere. It can occur in your organs or even in arteries as
they carry the bacteria through the body. Inflamed arteries

bring a greater risk of blockage, increasing your chances of heart attack or stroke. If you are a smoker, you are at even greater risk. Over 50 percent of smokers have periodontal disease, and, as we know, they have increased risk for any number of other diseases as well, giving them a double whammy. In addition, about twenty-eight thousand people a year are diagnosed with mouth cancer; early detection through dental examinations saves lives. When researchers looked at an overview of people's health as they age, they found a direct correlation between a history of good dental care and continuing overall health. People who did not maintain their teeth when they were younger had a much higher chance of developing chronic conditions when older.

For those reasons, it is never too late to start caring for your teeth. That means flossing and brushing and visiting the dentist. The drills, needles, and overall anxiety of dental work can be off-putting, but dental offices have changed a lot over the past twenty years, and dentists have all sorts of tricks to make the experience more pleasant: earphones, televisions, and techniques that can reduce the potential for pain to practically zero.

Unfortunately, sophisticated dental work can be extremely expensive. It's estimated that 108 million Americans do not have dental insurance—that's more than a third of the population. The cost and the fear factor cause many people to forego dental care until their throbbing molar is driving them to the brink of suicide. At that point, they're looking at either getting the tooth pulled or the alternative: root canal and crown or some other pricey procedure. In the long run, it makes more sense to visit a dentist regularly. If cost is a problem, explore discount insurance plans, low-cost clinics, or discounted care offered by dental schools in your area.

 ODD ARCHIVES ─────────────────

By the year 2000 there will be pills that cure phobias. Fear of heights, crowds, strangers, elevators, closed-in places, even fear of flying will be a thing of the past.

—*Encounters with the Future,* by Marvin Cetron
and Thomas O'Toole, 1982

WHAT'S BETTER FOR ME, COFFEE OR RED WINE?

Coffee beats red wine in the health derby, if only because its advantages have been more thoroughly studied. Coffee's proven benefits are its ability to boost memory and mental performance, increase alertness, and elevate mood. Anyone who drinks the stuff can confirm those findings, but because coffee seems too good to be true, it has been tested and retested over the past decade. Fears about the brew's health risks, based on early studies that showed a possible link to bladder cancer, high blood pressure, and a few other maladies, have now been refuted. Coffee may even protect against some diseases, including Parkinson's, diabetes, Alzheimer's, gallstones, depression, and liver disease. However, those benefits have not been proven.

Coffee's disadvantages are that it can temporarily elevate blood pressure and irritate the lining of the stomach. The caffeine, oils, and acids in coffee all may contribute to stomach irritation, and decaf has the same effect as regular. People with ulcers are always advised to stop drinking coffee (and alcohol). After the ulcer clears up, you may be able to indulge again.

Red wine has long been rumored to reduce the risk of heart disease. It contains flavonoids and other antioxidants, which might lead to a protective effect, but research has not yet borne this out. Among the populations who regularly drink red wine—most famously, the French—it has not been possible to prove that it was wine and no other factor that resulted in lower rates of heart disease. The American Heart Association (AHA) points out, with a slight edge of hysteria, that "drinking more alcohol increases such dangers as alcoholism, high blood pressure, obesity, stroke, breast cancer, suicide and accidents. . . . The American Heart Association cautions people *not* to start drinking . . . if they do not already drink alcohol." Besides, they say, if antioxidants prove to be beneficial, you can get them from fruits, vegetables, and red grape juice.

In 2007, Dutch researchers presented encouraging new findings about wine at an AHA conference. For forty years, beginning in 1960, they tracked the wine intake of 1,373 men and found that drinking wine (optimally, half a glass) was associated with lower rates of death from cardiovascular and overall causes. Drinking beer or spirits did not provide the same level of protection. Women were not included in the study.

Another interesting development occurred in 2005, when the Reykjavik Eye Study found that red wine might reduce the risk of cataracts: "Moderate wine drinkers had a 50% reduced incidence of cortical cataract and just less than half the risk for nuclear cataract when compared to the normal population." Other studies have shown red wine to have a chemopreventive effect against breast cancer: Researchers estimated that a single four-ounce glass a day would do the trick. While all this is promising, it is not backed by enough scientific study to qualify red wine as an honest-to-god health drink. However, if you enjoy a glass at dinner and are not at risk for the litany of ills spelled out by the AHA, it seems like a relatively safe choice.

WHO SHRINKS AND WHO DOESN'T?

It is common for people to shrink about 0.4 inch every ten years after the age of 40. By the time we are past 70, most of us will lose anywhere from one to three inches. Osteoporosis accounts for much of the height loss in women. It causes the bones to become porous and the vertebrae in the spine to compress from the weight of the body. But osteoporosis isn't the only factor contributing to old-age shrinkage. The intervertebral disks, which are pads between the vertebrae, grow thinner and drier with age. As they do, the space between the vertebrae shrinks, making the spine shorter. The muscles that hold the spine in place also play a role in maintaining height. If they become weak, the spine will start to slump. Finally, some people lose as much as three-fourths of an inch due to fallen arches in their feet.

In 2006, a group of researchers out of London published a study that revealed some unsettling correlations between height loss and mortality in men. After following 4,213 men for twenty years, they found that those who lost three centimeters (1.18 inches) or more were about 64 percent more likely to die from cardiovascular and respiratory conditions than men who shrank one centimeter (0.39 inch) or less. They could not tell why this is so, only that the connection exists. It could be that an underlying disorder is causing both the bone loss and the heart and respiratory conditions, or it could be that some of the problems brought on by a slumping spine, such as difficulty breathing and digesting food, set off a chain reaction of poor eating habits, weight loss, and other factors that contribute to the higher mortality rate.

What can help? Cue the familiar refrain: exercise. Weight-bearing exercise builds bone, slows bone loss, strengthens weak back muscles, stretches the spine, and helps improve posture. There are drugs that will help prevent osteoporosis, but some have risks that many women deem unacceptable. Vitamin and mineral supplements combined with weight-bearing exercises are a safer way to go. The younger you are when you start, the better your chance of maintaining your height.

WHAT ARE THE MOST COMMON INJURIES OF PEOPLE OVER 50?

While exercise is unquestionably beneficial to our well-being and is possibly the most potent weapon against disease, our 50-plus bodies are not the workout machines of yore. They are slowly wearing down, the parts have less padding, and the ligaments and bones tear and fracture more easily. None of that is difficult to adjust to. You simply do less strenuous exercises, replacing body-punishing sports such as football, soccer, and squash with activities like swimming, biking, hiking, and weight training. Tennis and golf occupy a middle ground—how they affect your body depends on how competitive you are and how often you play. Many seniors play golf and tennis into their eighties. However, because they tend to play so often, they increase their chances of getting injured while doing so. This is especially true of golf.

The hardest part about changing one's activities when you hit 40 or 50 is adjusting to the idea of yourself as being more breakable. Many midlifers work at desk jobs all week and on Saturday attack the basketball court or yoga mat with the zeal of a thirty-year-old. If they sustain an injury in the process, it is most likely to be one of the following.

Torn rotator cuff. The rotator cuff is a group of four tendons that stabilizes the shoulder joint. They attach to four muscles that enable your shoulder to move upward and around. Aging degrades this area and makes it more vulnerable to becoming inflamed, leading to tendonitis. If the tendonitis becomes severe, it can wear through the tendon, causing a tear in the cuff. Repetitive upward motions are often the root of the problem, and those typically happen while playing sports, for instance shooting a basketball, serving a tennis ball, or pitching a baseball. In these cases, you will probably feel pain and weakness for a long time before the cuff actually tears. If you are smart, you will halt the repetitive activity and go to a doctor. Tendonitis can be treated with cold therapy, pain medications, and physical therapy to strengthen the area. If you treat it early, you can avoid tearing the rotator cuff.

Occasionally people tear their rotator cuff while lifting a heavy item. If you hear a pop and feel sudden intense pain in your shoulder, that's a clue. It's called an acute rotator cuff tear (as opposed to the chronic rotator cuff tear described above). You will be at the doctor's soon afterward. Pain management, physical therapy, and surgery (as a last resort) may alleviate the problem.

Achilles' tendon rupture. The strongest tendon in the body, the Achilles stretches from your calf muscle to your heel bone. If you overextend it, it can tear or rupture. It's not uncommon to hear a popping sound when the tendon snaps, and to feel intense pain, as if you have been kicked or shot. Ruptures may be partial or complete. If you completely rupture the tendon, it will need to be stitched back together surgically. If the tear is partial, it may reattach itself, but you'll need to wear a cast or boot to hold your foot at the proper angle. The people most at risk for this injury are weekend warriors aged 30 to 50. Additional risk factors include starting a new activity or abruptly changing your training, intensity, or activity level.

Knee injury. Joints are especially susceptible to problems as we get older, because the natural cushioning that surrounds them becomes depleted and less cushy. The knee is the largest joint in the body and carries the most weight. Thus everything surrounding it is vulnerable to injury: the hamstring and quadriceps muscles that bend it back and forth, the cartilage that covers the ends of the bones, and the tendons and ligaments that connect the muscles and bones to one another.

Wrist or forearm fracture. Women suffer these more often than men, because they are more prone to osteoporosis. Fractures such as these, which are due to weakened bones, are called frailty fractures. They are usually the result of minor accidents, such as bracing a fall with your palm, rather than sports-related activities.

Yoga injury. Yoga postures can be especially treacherous for the weekend warrior. If an out-of-shape student meets up with an inexperienced teacher, disaster may result. Writing in *Yoga Journal,* Carol Krucoff lists typical injuries as ranging from "torn cartilage in the knees to joint problems from overly aggressive adjustments to sprained necks caused from 'the domino effect' of being knocked over by classmates while doing *shirsasana* (headstand)." The riskiest postures, she notes, are those that involve a seated, straight-leg forward bend that includes a twist. For the over-forty crowd, the posture that causes the most injuries is the shoulderstand.

EXPERT INPUT ─────────────────

Nina Moore, Fitness Expert

Nina Moore has been a fitness professional for more than fifteen years. A former elite athlete who ran track and field, Ms. Moore transitioned to the physical fitness industry when she was in her midthirties. She works at the Sports Club LA, a sports and fitness complex in West Los Angeles.

Who are your typical clients?
I train a variety of people, from your "household engineer" to professional athletes. Eighty percent of them are 40 and older. We're a high-end health club, and those are the people who can usually afford our services.

What prompts people to hire a trainer?
They're typically motivated either by a general health issue—their doctor told them they need to lower their blood pressure or cholesterol—or they are recovering from a specific injury. And people always want to lose weight and work on those five or ten pounds that seem to elude everybody. What often happens is that, as women reach middle age, their hormones change, and that adds an element they can't control by just doing the same thing they've always done. Someone who's been running five miles a day all her life suddenly gains a little weight around the middle, and running won't take it off. That's a motivating factor for her to come in and learn new ways to jump-start her metabolism

What expectations are realistic at 50? Is it reasonable to want to look like we did at 35?
Everybody has a different genetic background, so it's impossible to have an expectation of what one should look like. What you want to do is be healthy, feel good, have a

reasonable ratio of body fat to lean muscle mass, and make sure that you're able to enjoy the things that you like to do. If you enjoy playing tennis, can you play reasonably well and stay healthy while doing it? That's my focus with people. As you go into your forties and fifties, what do you want to do for fun? What are the things that bring you pleasure? Those are the activities you want to train for.

What psychological pitfalls have you noticed in clients who set out to reach a fitness goal?
People start off very enthusiastically, highly motivated, and that wanes at about week six, seven, or eight. One of the benefits of working with a trainer is that he or she can keep you motivated when you plateau, and everybody plateaus. You get to a point where, no matter what you're doing, it doesn't seem like you can lose that pound or two. A trainer can show you how to change your program and move off the plateau.

What goals do you encourage clients to have, other than losing weight?
My overriding goal with every client is that they have good health, and that doesn't always translate into pounds lost. It can be turning two or three pounds of fat into muscle. Their weight may not change, but the composition of the weight changes, which is better.

What is your first priority with new clients?
Posture. Good posture is the most fundamental part of having a healthy body. So when clients first come to see

me, I take a careful assessment of their posture and create a program that will restore their body's natural balance. I give them two or three specific areas to work on at a time, so they don't get overwhelmed.

What physical problems do your clients most frequently need help with?
Lower back pain. That's the number one complaint with most people. I also see a lot of neck and shoulder stress and stiffness, and some tennis elbow, but mostly it's lower back pain. That's because so many of us have poor posture.

What strategies do you use to keep your clients motivated?
I usually ask them to pick something they'd like to do that they have never done before. That's a great motivator. If you've never run a 5K, maybe you decide you want to do that, and we'll work toward that goal.

Are there any patterns you've seen in the attitudes among your midlife clients?
One of the good things is that our generation—40- and 50-year-olds—is becoming much more aware of the importance of maintaining good health. People are becoming active at a younger age. Working out is just a part of your life, like brushing your teeth. Society has become more accepting of it. There used to be a lot of weekend warriors, and then there were people who simply didn't place a high priority on exercise. They were chasing their careers,

climbing the corporate ladder, and that was the focus. Now we understand that, even though you may obtain a high level of success professionally, if you can't enjoy doing the things you like to do, it's all for naught.

What if you can't afford to hire a trainer indefinitely?
Try to be consistent for the first six weeks, minimum. If you can meet with your trainer twice a week for six weeks, that's great. Then you can go to once a week, then every other week. What you want to do is build a program. If your trainer is doing a good job, you'll become educated, and you'll know what you're supposed to do and why it is important for you to be doing those particular exercises. The trainer should create a program for you that is a well-thought-out plan that assists you in achieving a healthier body. You can come back, say, every six weeks for updates. Think of it as a tune-up for your body. The program adjusts as you make gains in strength, flexibility, and cardiovascular capacity, and it should also evolve with your goals.

What are the current trends in exercise?
People are starting to train the whole body rather than working on individual body parts. They're doing functional movements that mimic the activities they enjoy. For instance, if I play tennis, a lot of my training will use muscles and movement patterns that mimic those used in tennis, so that as I'm training, my body is becoming stronger while moving and I'm becoming a better player.

So the ideal is to pick a sport or activity that you like and couple it with a workout that reinforces it?
Absolutely. If you pick an activity that you really enjoy doing and your training is allowing you to do it better, longer, to increase your enjoyment, then you're going to be a lot more excited about training.

What words of wisdom do you have for people who have never joined a health club or been into exercise?
It's never too late to get in the game. If you are not an exerciser, it's easy to become an exerciser. Just start at a low level. I encourage people to work with trainers. Treat yourself! Go in and find someone who's knowledgeable and can teach you. Our job as trainers is to educate our clients, and my philosophy is: Train for life. Train to live the life that you want to live and then go out and do it!

WHY DO ARCHES FALL?

Some people are born with fallen arches, or flat feet. Others get the condition later in life, especially if they have spent many years working on their feet or in high heels. In either case, the extra strain on the foot causes the tendons that hold the arch in place to become inflamed, weaken, or to tear. When this happens the tendon stretches and the arch falls.

The main support structure for the arch is the posterior tibial tendon, which runs behind the inside bump on the ankle, across the instep, and into the bottom of the foot. Trouble can occur when a woman wears high heels because the angle of the foot affects the Achilles tendon, which runs up the back of the ankle. The foot's structure is altered each day by high heels, and the posterior tibial tendon may try to compensate for the stress, eventually breaking down. People who are on their feet every day stress the tibial tendon from overuse. The same happens with people who are obese. Other causes can include poor circulation, arthritis, or an injury to the ankle or foot.

Your arches may be slipping if your feet are often achy, your ankles hurt when you walk on uneven surfaces or up stairs, or if you have swelling on the inside of the ankle or lower leg. Another symptom: It's hard for you to move your heel or midfoot around or to stand on your heels. Treatment runs the gamut from changing your shoes or wearing orthotics (custom foot supports) all the way through surgery.

ARE MY FEET GETTING BIGGER, OR ARE SHOES GETTING SMALLER?

Sometimes having flat feet will make a person's foot longer, but regardless of whether or not they have that condition, most people will gain a full shoe size by the time they are fifty. After fifty years of use, you wear out about half the natural padding under the balls of your feet, according to a 2005 report published in the *New York Times*. The foot gets not only longer but also wider, especially in the forefoot.

The shoe dilemma is more complicated than simply growing a size, however. Shoe sizes have become deregulated, so to speak, over the past decade or so. "As far as we know, there are no standards that the industry itself follows," said Susan Lapetina, a spokeswoman for the American Apparel and Footwear Association, in an article for the *Pittsburgh Post-Gazette*. "There are no hard-and-fast rules. There's no sizing chart." If you were reliably a size 7 all your life but now fit into anything from a 6½ to an 8, that's why. And if you have always been hard to fit, it's not your imagination that things are getting worse. Nowadays there are very few styles available in sizes other than 6 to 10 medium for women and 8 to 10½ for men. People who can't find size 11 must squeeze their feet into a 10½, and people with wide feet are forced buy shoes that are too large. Blisters, bunions, and a slew of other foot problems are the price one pays for wearing shoes that don't fit properly. Those problems, with their painful bumps and inflammation, may cause you to feel comfortable only in shoes that are larger than the ones you used to buy.

The fact is that everyone's feet are getting bigger, not just people who are 50-plus. According to Dr. William Rossi, a shoe historian, podiatrist, and author of *The Professional Shoe Fitting Manual*, in the year 1900 the average American woman wore a size 3½ or 4. By the 1940s she wore a 5½, and by the 1970s, a 7½. Right now the average is an 8. Men have gone from an average size 6 in the 1700s to 9½ today. As the average foot has gotten larger, so has the demand for shoes at the upper end of the scale—for example, women's shoes in sizes 10, 11, and 12.

The shoe industry is not bothering to meet the growing demand for larger and wider sizes or for anything outside the average range that department stores prefer to stock. Writing in slate.com, Jennifer Howard (size 11 narrow) summed up the mall shoe-shopping experience this way: "The standard 5 to 10 size range becomes a self-fulfilling prophecy; they don't stock many so-called plus sizes, so big-footed people learn not to endure the humiliation of shopping there, which means that the stores can say there's no demand. Adding insult to unavailability, a lot of retailers apparently cling to the idea that the big-shoe buyer is either a fashion-blind biddy with corns or a hard-luck case who can barely afford the box her knockoff Nikes come in."

Women who want stylish shoes in not-so-average sizes do have a few online options. Designershoes.com stocks sizes 6 to 15 and specializes in large sizes; nordstrom.com has sizes 4 to 15; bamason.com has plenty of petite sizes; and zappo.com has sizes 3 to 15, although the selection is thin at the extreme ends of the scale.

No discussion of shoe size would be entirely complete without a brief consideration of the myth that a man's shoe size relates to the size of that other important appendage. Three scientific studies have been done to test the theory, the most recent one published in the October 2002 edition of the *British Journal of Urology International*. One of the earlier studies had found no correlation between shoe size and penis length; the other found a weak correlation. But in the previous studies, mused the authors, "All measurements were self-recorded and therefore are subject to bias." For their own work, they put the measuring tape in the hands of objective professionals: "[The] stretched penile length is a valid estimate of erect length. . . . All lengths were measured by two urologists and recorded to the nearest 0.5 cm." The results: "There was no statistically significant correlation between shoe size and stretched penile length."

WHY DO BONES CREAK?

There is a technical name for creaking bones: crepitation, from the Latin verb *crepare,* meaning to crackle (not from the same root as *decrepit,* surprisingly). Unless you are experiencing pain along with the creaking, it's probably nothing to worry about. The sound commonly comes from the knee joint and is caused by surfaces rubbing against each other, by ligaments coming into contact, or by pressure changes in the synovial fluid that surrounds the joint.

If you do feel pain when your bones creak, it could be an early sign of osteoarthritis. This condition occurs when cartilage between the bones wears away and the bones rub against each other. The lack of healthy cartilage may also cause the bones to slide out of their correct position. You'll feel stiffness, have difficulty moving, and hear the creak of the weary, thickened joint. Other painful conditions may also cause your bones to creak and crackle. These include loose fragments in the joint and torn meniscus cartilage, which sometimes makes a clicking sound. In all cases of creaking bones, the general rule is, if it hurts, see a doctor.

DO I NEED CENTRUM SILVER?

In 1990, when Centrum Silver first launched a special vitamin for seniors, its advertising agency assumed that people over 50 would have no problem being lumped in with 60- and 70-year-olds. They thought we'd identify with wind-blown, canoeing graybeards and that we'd appreciate being thought of as "silver." How many silver-haired 50-year-old women do you know? The ad irritated midlifers back then, and its reputation as a pill for old fogies remains to this day. Their current advertising features only a few gray heads, but the denizens of Planet Centrum still favor outdoor exercise that, judging from their batty grins, is wildly satisfying.

The concept behind Centrum Silver and other multivitamins aimed at the 50-plus crowd is that our nutritional needs are different than those of younger adults. This is true for the following vitamins and minerals:

Vitamin B12. After 50, some people (about 30 percent) have difficulty absorbing B12, a vitamin that helps maintain nerve cells and red blood cells. A B12 deficiency can result in anemia, symptoms of which include feeling tired and listless and having poor resistance to infection. Adults over 50 need 2.4 micrograms a day. Most multivitamins contain this amount of B12.

Vitamin D. Our skin formulates vitamin D from sunlight, and its ability to do so decreases with age. In addition, our exposure to sunlight is often limited by the couch/car/cubicle nature of our existence and the fact that we smear so much sunscreen on our skin when we do venture outdoors. The recommended daily allowance of vitamin D is set at 400 IU (International Units), which is the amount contained in most multivitamins. However, many health experts are now advising people to take as much as 1000 IU.

Vitamin D strengthens bones and helps prevent osteoporosis. There is some evidence that it may protect against breast, colon, ovarian, and prostate cancer. Even if those findings do not pan out, we still need our D. In 2004, a federally funded national health survey found that many Americans were deficient in the vitamin, especially people with dark skin, those who get very little natural sunlight, and the elderly. You can get vitamin D in foods such as milk, herring, and sardines, but most adults are not eager to drink tall glasses of milk or gobble canned fish, so a supplement is useful.

Calcium. All women should get extra calcium to protect their bones, and both men and women over 50 should get 1,200 to 1,500 milligrams a day. No multivitamins, including Centrum Silver, contain this much calcium, because it would make the pill too large.

Iron. Women and men over 50 need less iron (especially women who are no longer losing iron with their monthly periods). We get enough iron from the foods we eat, unless we specifically have an iron deficiency. Centrum Silver and other 50-plus vitamins do not contain iron.

In theory, there is no advantage to taking Centrum Silver or any of the other boomer-targeted multivitamins. A generic multivitamin with no iron should serve your purposes just as well, as long as you supplement it with enough calcium and vitamin D to meet the levels suggested above. However, there is some question as to whether the generics actually provide the vitamins they purport to. Many generic multis are marked USP, which means that the vitamins meet the standards of the U.S. Pharmacopeia. Brand-name multis often do not carry the USP label because the manufacturers rely on name recognition to reassure consumers of the product's quality.

Consumer Reports was curious about the vitamin content of generic versus brand-name multivitamins, so in 2004 they surveyed eighteen multis purchased from dollar stores and other discount centers and compared them to brand-name multis. They reported that "eight failed to meet the label claim for one or more nutrients, and three of those eight didn't dissolve properly. Moreover, three of the substandard products said USP on the label. . . . In contrast, major multivitamin brands proved so reliable the last time we tested them that we didn't bother evaluating more than two such brands this time. Those products, Centrum From A to Zinc and Bayer One-A-Day Maximum, did indeed meet their label claims and were free of the tested contaminants.

"Even if the cut-rate multivitamins were reliable, they offer savings of only about $3 to $21 a year over name-brand products; even less, if any, over major store brands. We recommend sticking to those better-known brands of multivitamins."

No amount of vitamins or supplements can take the place of a diet that is rich in fruits, vegetables, and whole grains. However, Americans of all ages tend to go on diets, eat junk food, neglect their bodies, or simply lack the time and energy to prepare healthy meals. Multivitamins, along with calcium and vitamin D supplements, are an excellent way for midlifers to fill in the nutritional gaps. The best time to take your multi is with a meal. If the pills are too big for you to comfortably swallow, invest a few dollars in a pill slicer, available at most pharmacies.

SHOULD I GET MY THYROID LEVELS TESTED?

Symptoms of thyroid imbalance can be alarmingly similar to symptoms of much more serious disorders. Fortunately, thyroid problems often are easy to manage. The thyroid is a small gland that lies in your neck just below your Adam's apple. It secretes a hormone called thyroxine, which helps regulate body temperature, growth, metabolism, and digestion. Thyroid levels that are too low (hypothyroidism) can cause symptoms such as fatigue, weight gain, constipation, dry skin and hair, heavy menstrual periods, feeling cold, and slowed thinking. If the levels are too high (hyperthyroidism), you may experience rapid heartbeat, weight loss, dizziness, irritability, nervousness, shakiness, fatigue, more frequent bowel movements, feeling hot, and shorter or lighter periods.

Because these symptoms often emerge slowly, thyroid conditions frequently go undiagnosed or misdiagnosed. If you suspect you might have a thyroid disorder, ask your doctor for a blood test that measures your levels of thyroid-stimulating hormone (TSH). In most cases, a pill a day will correct the problem.

WHICH MEDICAL TESTS ARE MUST-HAVES AFTER 50?

There is currently some debate about how many tests anyone really needs and whether or not Americans have gone test-crazy. However, just about everyone agrees that the following tests should be on your to-do list if you are over 50. Your family health history may prompt your doctor to recommend other tests as well.

MEN

Blood pressure. Every one to two years.

Cholesterol. Every five years.

Colonoscopy (colorectal cancer screening). At age 50 and every ten years thereafter.

Diabetes. Every five years.

Eyesight. At 50, and then according to your doctor's recommendation. As you get older you become more susceptible to glaucoma, macular degeneration, and cataracts. Early detection is key to maintaining good vision throughout your life.

Prostate cancer. The American Cancer Society recommends being screened every year beginning at age 50, but this view is not shared by everyone. More than most tests, prostate cancer screening (a digital rectal exam and a PSA blood test) can result in confusing, inaccurate results and false positives, which in turn may lead to unnecessary biopsies, treatment, and anxiety. African-American men and those with a family history of prostate cancer are at greater risk for the disease. Discuss your situation with your doctor, and then decide whether to have the test.

WOMEN

Blood pressure. Every one to two years.

Bone density. At 65, or at age 60 if you weigh less than 155 pounds.

Cholesterol. Every five years.

Colonoscopy (colorectal cancer screening). At age 50 and every ten years thereafter.

Diabetes. Every five years.

Eyesight. At 50, and then according to your doctor's recommendation. As you get older you become more susceptible to glaucoma, macular degeneration, and cataracts. Early detection is key to maintaining good vision throughout your life.

Mammogram. At 50 and every one to two years thereafter.

Pap smear. Every one to two years.

SOMETIMES I FEEL LIKE I'VE GOT TO PEE, BUT WHEN I TRY, I CAN'T. WHY?

The problem, which afflicts about half of all men 50 and older, can often be traced to *benign prostatic hyperplasia* (BPH). Translation: a nonthreatening, noncancerous enlargement of the prostate gland. The prostate is located between the bladder, where urine is stored, and the urethra, the tube that carries urine out of the body. It is common for the prostate to get bigger as men get older, and if it gets big enough to press against the urethra, it can cause the flow of urine to become weaker and slower.

A lot of men suffer from BPH, but surveys have found that only 10 percent of them require medical or surgical treatment. In about a third of the mild cases, symptoms clear up on their own. For some men, BPH is merely irritating and embarrassing. For others it can become debilitating, as constant bathroom breaks ruin their sleep and interfere with their daily activities.

Luckily, there are some helpful treatments for the condition. Unluckily, one of the most common of these is the drug finasteride (Proscar). Finasteride is sold under the name Propecia when it is prescribed to treat hair loss in men; you can read more about it and its side effects in chapter 4, "Hair." The side effects can be severe and may include sexual dysfunction, so research it carefully and ask your doctor about alternatives before agreeing to take it. The standard dosage of Proscar is five times that of Propecia. Not all men will suffer from finasteride's nastier side effects, but you should be aware of them. Your doctor may prescribe dutasteride (Avodart) instead of finasteride; it belongs to the same family and causes the same side effects. The drugs work by blocking a hormone that causes the prostate to enlarge. They are not effective for everyone, but they do bring significant relief to some.

Doctors also prescribe alpha blockers for men with BPH. These are used to treat high blood pressure but may also alleviate BPH symptoms, even in men whose blood pressure is normal. Alpha blockers relax the muscles in the bladder, which increases the flow of urine. Side effects may include dizziness, fatigue, and lightheadedness. A 2003 study published in the *New England Journal of Medicine* found that taking an alpha blocker and finasteride in tandem was more effective than taking either one alone.

If medications don't help your symptoms, there are surgical procedures that may. These range from techniques that use lasers, microwaves, or radio waves to remove excess tissue around the prostate gland, to a more traditional and invasive surgery called TURP (transurethral resection of the prostate), which involves removing larger portions of the gland. A possible side effect of TURP is erectile dysfunction, which happens to 5 to 10 percent of the men who undergo the procedure.

What about herbal remedies? Saw palmetto is sometimes touted as a treatment for BPH. In 2006, the *New England Journal of Medicine* published the results of a double-blind trial using saw palmetto. The herb was a bust—it performed no better than the placebo. On the positive side, with millions of men turning 50 each year, researchers are eager to discover better methods of treating BPH.

WHAT'S WITH THE PEEING WHEN I SNEEZE?

Would you believe there are support groups for this? And you thought AA meetings were boring. If you suffer from stress incontinence—the medical term for urinating when you sneeze, laugh, or otherwise put pressure on your bladder—the National Association for Continence (NAFC) can point you to a group near you. The fact that there are support groups for the condition can only mean two things: A lot of people have it, and most of them are women. According to the NAFC, about 25 million adults suffer from some kind of urinary incontinence, and 75 to 80 percent of them are female. Severe cases can interfere with one's activities, sex life, or sleep.

While stress incontinence is not a result of aging per se, it can become a problem in midlife, because that is when the muscles of the pelvic floor, which support the bladder, and the urinary sphincter, which controls the release of urine, may become weaker. Stress incontinence is one condition you can't blame on your evil ways. It is not preventable, and it has little to do with lifestyle choices. Many women first encounter the condition when they become mothers, if their pelvic floor muscles or urinary sphincter were damaged during delivery. In some cases the damage sustained at that time doesn't cause incontinence until many years later. Obesity can be a contributing factor to the condition as well. Men who have had their prostate gland removed may develop stress incontinence, because the prostate helps support the urethra.

There are many strategies women can employ to correct or control the problem. First, see a doctor to get a proper diagnosis and rule out possible causes such as urinary tract infection. The doctor may suggest that you cut down on caffeine and alcohol, which exacerbate the symptoms. You may be advised to do Kegels, the butt-clenching exercises pregnant women do to strengthen their pelvic floor. In addition, there are vaginal weighted cones—sort of like free weights for your vagina—you can insert to force yourself to keep clenched and build up those pelvic muscles. Other devices, such as bladder-neck supports and urethral plugs, can be used to temporarily prevent leakage.

For both men and women, surgical procedures can lift, tighten, or plump up with collagen the weakened areas that are causing the problem. However, do not even think about undergoing such a procedure without making sure your surgeon is extremely experienced. Go to the forums at www.nafc.org if you need to be convinced.

WHAT ON EARTH HAS HAPPENED TO MY DIGESTIVE SYSTEM?

All the body's systems slow down a little as you age, and that includes the digestive system. This means that food moves more slowly through the digestive tract, a situation made worse if you don't exercise. The sluggish journey through upper and lower intestines can lead to constipation. In addition, after age forty, the esophageal muscles that squeeze food down your esophagus to the stomach start to weaken. As a result, stomach acids may splash back up into the esophagus, a condition called acid reflux. Acid reflux causes heartburn.

A slothful digestive tract may also be to blame for the bloating and gas you may suffer when eating food you once gobbled with abandon, such as onions, strawberries, or tomatoes. Beano may provide relief. It contains a natural enzyme that helps your system break down complex sugars in "gassy" foods such as vegetables, grains, and beans. The key is to take the right amount of Beano with your food—the manufacturer suggests about three tablets or fifteen drops at an average meal. The Beano and the food should reach your stomach at the same time in order for the enzyme to do its work.

Another age-related intestinal problem is diverticulosis, which usually strikes after 40. It occurs in the colon (large intestine) and is the penalty for a lifetime of eating processed foods with little fiber or nutritional value. Fiber promotes the movement of food through your intestines and helps create soft stools that pass easily though the colon. Low-fiber processed foods form into hard, dry stools that are difficult to pass. All the years of straining to push them through can weaken the walls of the colon and cause little pouches called diverticula to form there. The condition can cause gas, cramping, and indigestion. Foods like nuts, seeds, and popcorn can get caught in the pouches, causing more pain.

Revolting, isn't it? Yet each of these conditions, if they are not serious enough to warrant medical intervention, can be improved by the good old duo of diet and exercise. Fresh fruits and vegetables, whole-grain breads and cereals, and lots of water are the foundation of digestive bliss. However, be sure to add the fiber slowly. Too much fiber in a digestive tract that isn't accustomed to it can lead to sudden intense gastrointestinal pain. I discovered that the hard way when I spent four days at a health resort that featured all-vegetarian cuisine. As I lay writhing in pain in the middle of the dirt-bike trail on day three, the guide casually mentioned that a lot of guests weren't used to all those grains and beans. It's a lesson I'll never forget.

IS IT POSSIBLE TO DEVELOP FOOD ALLERGIES IN YOUR FIFTIES?

Although relatively few adults have food allergies—roughly 2 percent, compared with about 7 percent of children—you can develop them at any time during your life. If you had allergies as a child, or if other people in your family have allergies, such as asthma, eczema, or hay fever, you may be more susceptible to food allergies now that you are grown. The foods that most commonly cause an allergic reaction in adults are shellfish, finned fish, and tree nuts, such as almonds, pecans, and walnuts.

For the past twenty years, a condition called oral-allergy syndrome has been on the rise among adults. It usually occurs in people who had pollen allergies in their youth, even if those earlier allergies have disappeared. Years later, when they are in their thirties or older, some will suddenly develop an allergy to tree fruits, tree nuts, or vegetables, such as celery or carrots. Typical responses are itching in the mouth, runny nose, watery eyes, and congestion.

No one knows why adults suddenly become allergic to certain foods. While a family history may predispose someone to develop allergies, it remains a mystery why one person will break out in hives after only a brief exposure to a particular food and another person will be able to eat it for twenty years and only then have a reaction.

Allergic reactions to food usually occur within fifteen to thirty minutes of eating the item. If symptoms arise an hour or two after the meal, it may be a food intolerance, not an allergy. In general, the sooner an allergic reaction begins, the more severe it will be. Symptoms of food allergies include:

- itching
- tingling
- swelling in the lips, tongue, or throat
- hives

- a rash
- cramps, upset stomach, or diarrhea
- stuffy nose, wheezing, feeling short of breath
- feeling dizzy or lightheaded

Occasionally people suffer from a life-threatening form of allergic reaction called *anaphylaxis*. It often occurs within minutes of eating the food, and symptoms can return one or two hours later. Signs of anaphylaxis include:

- rapid swelling of throat and tongue
- faintness or fainting
- difficulty breathing, wheezing
- nausea or vomiting

Call 911 *immediately* if you have any of these symptoms. Do not try to drive yourself to the nearest emergency room. Allergic reactions can escalate quickly, and the paramedics in the ambulance may need to administer a life-saving shot of epinephrine (which you will carry with you in a preloaded syringe from that day forward).

WHAT'S THE DIFFERENCE BETWEEN ARTERIOSCLEROSIS AND ATHEROSCLEROSIS?

Arteriosclerosis is hardening of the arteries, and atherosclerosis is the most common form of it, caused by a buildup of fatty deposits (plaques) on the inside wall of the arteries. Healthy arteries are flexible, whereas those with arteriosclerosis are thick and stiff. The hardened, narrowed arteries have trouble delivering enough oxygen and nutrients to the body's muscles. The most commonly affected arteries are those in the heart, brain, kidneys, abdominal aorta, and legs. Hardened arteries cause heart attacks, angina, strokes, and aneurysms. They can also impede the circulation to your arms and legs, a condition called peripheral arterial disease.

Signs that you may be developing arteriosclerosis include chest pain, sudden numbness, weakness, dizziness, leg pain when exercising, and erectile dysfunction. It's crucial that you see a doctor if you're experiencing any of these, because a symptom in one area, for instance leg pain, could very well mean that you have hardened arteries elsewhere in your body and are at risk for a heart attack or stroke.

WHAT IS "BIOLOGICAL AGE"?

"Fact: Your RealAge is the biological age of your body based on over 100 factors—many that you control."

Another fact: once a company coins a term like RealAge, they can define it any way they like and then call it a fact. RealAge, Inc., is "a consumer-health media company and provider of personalized health information and management tools. These tools motivate health-conscious people like you to look, feel, and actually be many years younger—to Live Life to the Youngest." In other words, the term *biological age* has been plucked from the scientific community and used to cash in on boomers' anxiety about getting older. If you redefine age itself, the theory goes, it's a short leap to deciding how old you want to be, popping a few vitamins, and then "actually being" it.

The antiaging Web site growyouthful.com, like many biological-age sites, offers a lengthy test designed to help you determine your body's "true" age. The site advises, "To answer a question like 'Delicate skin, bruises easily?' or 'Crows feet around your eyes?' compare your skin to the perfect skin of a healthy young person." Other quizzes instruct you to gauge how many gray hairs you have, measure the flabby part of your arm between the shoulder and elbow, divide your waist measurement by your hip measurement, and blow out a candle. (Blowing out your brains might be a more appealing prospect after a hundred-plus questions like these.) The ultimate goal is usually to get you to buy nutritional supplements, yoga classes, skin cream, or any of the thousands of antiaging products available to the nervous midlifer.

The concept of biological age isn't a recent phenomenon. It has intrigued the medical community since 1947, when the first efforts were made to measure "true age." Since that time, researchers have struggled to find a way to synthesize the myriad factors that affect the rate at which an individual's body begins to deteriorate. In 1994, a paper published in *Gerontology* outlined an attempt to solve nine of the thorniest problems. Most involved methods of measuring biological age: What age do you begin with? How long do you study the group? Whom do you study? What about people who get a disease or are hurt in an accident? Two problems had to do with the inherent quirkiness of the human body: Different organs age at different rates, and individuals age at different rates at different times. The challenge of wrestling all these factors into a usable scale was daunting. The study's authors concluded that other researchers should "extend our body of knowledge by further careful studies."

Doctors are interested in biological age so they can better determine who is a good risk for surgery and other medical treatments and—the holy grail—so they can predict when an individual is likely to die. Physicians know that some people who are 70 appear to be 60, while others could pass for 80. "Chronological age since birth gives little indication of how biologically 'old' a patient really is," noted a group of doctors in the *Journal of the Royal Society of Medicine* in 2001. When deciding whether to perform surgery, doctors will examine the patient, ask questions about his or her lifestyle and performance of daily tasks, and use a computer program to calculate the patient's medical history and status. A reliable tool for determining true biological age would be a great help to these physicians, but so far such a tool eludes them.

In 2002, the editors at *Scientific American* summarized the biological-age conundrum, and no major breakthroughs have occurred since that time: "Scientists believe that random damage that occurs within cells and among extracellular molecules are responsible for many of the age-related changes that are observed in organisms. In addition, for organisms that reproduce sexually, including humans, each individual is genetically unique. As such, the rate of aging also varies from individual to individual. Despite intensive study, scientists have not been able to discover reliable measures of the processes that contribute to aging. For these reasons, any claim that a person's biological or 'real age' can currently be measured, let alone modified, by any means must be regarded as entertainment, not science."

WHAT IS THE AVERAGE WEIGHT OF PEOPLE OVER 50? WHAT IS "IDEAL"?

There are a number of theories about whether weight gain is inevitable after 50. For women, the controversy involves whether or not the loss of estrogen after menopause causes fat cells to proliferate around the midsection. The idea was introduced by Debra Waterhouse in her book, *Outsmarting the Midlife Fat Cell* (Hyperion, 1999). In it she explains that when a woman enters perimenopause, her body's fat cells increase in size, number, and the ability to store fat. The body's goal is to have the fat cells produce estrogen, because the ovaries will no longer be doing so. The fat cells around the waist are best at producing estrogen, according to Waterhouse, so that's where the cells are most likely to multiply.

Other researchers have found that gaining weight in midlife is not a foregone conclusion but has more to do with getting lazier and wealthier. You have the money to buy tasty restaurant meals, you no longer need to chase toddlers around the house, and you're tired of depriving yourself, so you eat more and move less. One study of 541 women age 42 to 50 found that they gained the same amount of weight whether or not they had entered menopause, which seems to support the theory that behavior, not hormones, are determining the gain.

But in the end, it doesn't matter why you're gaining

weight. The solution remains the same litany you've heard all your life: Eat less. Exercise more. Eat healthier foods. Weight-train. I could elaborate, but you know the drill. Instead, let's take a look at what everybody *really* weighs and what the experts say about it.

For many years, doctors and dieticians relied on Metropolitan Life Insurance Company's tables to determine the optimum height and weight for individuals. These tables were on the chart posted on your doctor's wall when you were a kid, and they may still be up there. The tables list height/weight ratios that MetLife calculated would result in the lowest mortality rates. In the public's mind, the MetLife weights have come to represent the ideal, even though MetLife never labeled them as such (they term them "desirable"). The original tables were published in 1943 and updated forty years later. They are widely reprinted on the Internet, usually accompanied by an indignant sentence or two about how the tables haven't been revised since 1983. But "we haven't *used* those tables since 1983," a MetLife PR specialist told me. Unfortunately, their influence lives on.

On the Web site hallsmd.com, Dr. Steven B. Halls explains that the MetLife table assumes people are wearing shoes with one-inch heels—a fact few are aware of. Although the table includes three frame sizes (small, medium, and large), Dr. Halls believes the figures give poor results for very short and very tall people, particularly the latter: "For very tall men and women, the MetLife tables suggest *impossibly* low weights." Keep that in mind if you're in the doctor's office and your eye falls upon an ancient MetLife table. When you realize that you should be looking at the weight for a height one inch taller than you actually are, it becomes a little less scary.

If the MetLife table is not accurate, how can we determine a healthy weight for our height? There are other charts that offer a range of desirable weights, but most physicians now prefer to calculate an individual's body mass index (BMI). BMI indicates your total body fat, which in turn is related to risk of disease and death, according to the National Institutes of Health (NIH). The BMI formula in pounds to inches is: weight multiplied by 704.5 divided by your height squared. (In kilograms to meters, it is simply your weight divided by your height squared.) Many Web sites offer BMI calculators to help you do the math. What is a *good* BMI number? Here is the score card:

Underweight = <18.5
Normal weight = 18.5–24.9
Overweight = 25.0–29.9
Obese = BMI of 30.0 or greater

There are limits to the BMI's accuracy: It may overestimate body fat in athletes and others who have a muscular build and underestimate body fat in the elderly and others who have lost muscle mass. And there are other factors that influence the number's usefulness as a guide to healthy weight. One is your waist circumference. The NIH decrees that a waistline of more than 40 inches in men and 35 inches in woman is "a good indicator of your abdominal fat which is another predictor of your risk for developing risk factors for heart disease and other diseases." Then the NIH goes on to list other tests that must be considered along with BMI score and waistline when calculating your healthy weight. The NIH recommends weight loss for people who have a BMI of 25 or greater *and* two or more of the following risks:

- high blood pressure (hypertension)
- high LDL cholesterol ("bad" cholesterol)
- low HDL cholesterol ("good" cholesterol)
- high triglycerides
- high blood glucose (sugar)
- family history of premature heart disease
- physical inactivity
- cigarette smoking

All of which means that your BMI score alone is not necessarily an accurate indicator of a healthy weight for you. That is fortunate, because the BMI scoring system is even less forgiving than the MetLife table. A five-foot-three-inch woman with a medium frame could weigh 121 to 135 pounds according to MetLife, and her big-boned sister could weigh up to 147. BMI does not differentiate between males and females, much less small, medium, and large frames. If you are five foot three and weigh more than 140, BMI scores you as overweight.

MEN: AVERAGE WEIGHT IN POUNDS, 2002

Age	20-39	40-59	60 and over
Caucasian	190	200	189
Hispanic	172	184	176
African American	189	191	187

MEN: AVERAGE HEIGHT IN INCHES, 2002

Age	20-39	40-59	60 and over
Caucasian	5'10"	5'10"	5'9"
Hispanic	5'7"	5'7"	5'6"
African American	5'10"	5'10"	5'9"

WOMEN: AVERAGE WEIGHT IN POUNDS, 2002

Age	20-39	40-59	60 and over
Caucasian	158	167	158
Hispanic	152	165	150
African American	179	189	176

WOMEN: AVERAGE HEIGHT IN INCHES, 2002

Age	20-39	40-59	60 and over
Caucasian	5'5"	5'5"	5'3"
Hispanic	5'2"	5'2"	5'1"
African American	5'5"	5'4"	5'3"

Once you have calculated your BMI, you may want to boost your spirits with a glimpse at what your fellow Americans weigh. The tables on page 124 are based on data from a National Health and Nutrition Examination Survey (NHANES) conducted in 1999–2002. They reveal the mean, or average, weight and height of American men and women (rounded to the nearest pound or inch).

The National Institutes of Health's Web site flatly states, "People who are overweight or obese have a greater chance of developing high blood pressure, high blood cholesterol or other lipid disorders, type 2 diabetes, heart disease, stroke, and certain cancers, and even a small weight loss (just 10 percent of your current weight) will help to lower your risk of developing those diseases."

That sounds definitive. It is worth noting that not everyone agrees with this assessment, especially as it concerns people who are overweight but not obese. In *The Gospel of Food,* sociologist Barry Glassner's study of Americans' love/hate relationship with eating, the author quotes a 1998 editorial by the physician editors of the *New England Journal of Medicine:* "Given the enormous social pressure to lose weight, one might suppose there is clear and overwhelming evidence of the risks of obesity and the benefits of weight loss. Unfortunately, the data linking overweight and death, as well as the data showing the beneficial effects of weight loss, are limited, fragmentary, and often ambiguous." The physicians noted that because of our fixation on losing weight, "many Americans are sacrificing their appreciation of one of the great pleasures of life—eating."

While it is clearly unwise to lead a slothful, gluttonous life, many health experts lament that women in particular have become obsessed with attaining "chart weight," whether the chart is the old MetLife table, a more recent version, or the BMI score. One advantage to getting older may be our ability to reason our way past weight hysteria and finally enjoy the occasional guilt-free crème brûlée.

four

HAIR

WHAT HAPPENS AT THE HAIR CLUB FOR MEN?
Somewhere along the road to middle age, Sy Sperling's ceaseless chant—"I'm not only the Hair Club president, I'm a *client!*"—begins to penetrate the ears of many American males. They may have snorted at Sy's infomercials all through their twenties; they may even have flipped past them during their thirties without pausing except to swiftly cross themselves. But at some point, their thumb will hesitate over the remote. They will run an uneasy hand through their hair and wonder for the first time, "What *is* the Hair Club?"

Sy Sperling began the Hair Club for Men in 1968, when he was 26 years old, divorced, overweight, and already balding. To remedy at least one of these date-deterring attributes, he got a hair weave. The results must have been spectacular, because Sperling decided to shuck his job selling swimming pools and open his own hair-replacement business. At that point, the focus of Hair Club for Men was on perfecting the hair weave, which was then the only alternative to toupees and transplants. His business grew at a reasonable rate until 1982, when the first Hair Club infomercial was aired. "We got 10,000 calls the first month,"

Sperling recalled in an interview with the *Los Angeles Times*. "Unbelievable response."

After the infomercial, Hair Clubs began sprouting up all across the United States. As of this writing, they have locations in thirty-six states, Canada, Nova Scotia, and Puerto Rico. Now officially called The Hair Club for Men and Women, they offer a full slate of hair-replacement services, from minoxidil-based products to transplants. But the soul of the company remains their hairpieces, or the Strand by Strand Bio-Matrix process, as they call it. According to the company's literature, the weave is "a matrix of crisscrossing, transparent fibers, fitted and shaped to the client's thinning area. It is virtually invisible, so it will take on the color of your skin. Anywhere you part the hair you will see your own scalp. More importantly, the matrix is porous. This is essential in that water, shampoo, heat, and sweat pass through the matrix giving your scalp the ability to 'breathe.' In the shower you can actually feel the water hitting your scalp. Your own hair can continue to grow unobstructed. . . .

"What this means is that when you brush your hair it all blends together. If someone were to touch your hair it would feel normal. Not only is the hair easy to style, but you don't have to worry about roughing it up. You can go swimming, biking, jogging, anywhere life takes you. This is your hair!"

The biomatrix process involves weaving real human hair onto a thin membrane about the thickness of a nylon stocking, only firmer. The membrane is molded to fit the part of the client's skull where the hair is thinning. It is glued in place using surgical glue, and it generally needs to be reattached by a Hair Club stylist every six weeks, when the glue begins to loosen. The maintenance schedule also depends on how quickly the client's real hair grows, because it needs to be cut to blend in with the hairpiece, or the assemblage begins to look a bit off.

The typical Hair Club waiting room features a thick binder full of testimonials from clients claiming they wore their hairpieces skiing, snorkeling, and on month-long African safaris, where the hair neither fell off nor aroused suspicion among their tent-mates. However, the look of the hairpieces varies widely from man to man. The Hair Club headquarters in Los Angeles is conspicuously full of people who aren't just employees, they're *clients*. On some, the false hair is all but impossible to discern. On others, it looks like a slightly more refined version of the good old toupee, the giveaway being that the texture of the hair on top of the head doesn't match the texture of the hair on the sides. The color and hairlines look natural, but the false hair sometimes appears to be spikier or curlier than the natural hair, and there may be a visible line where the two overlap.

The initial cost of a Hair Club hairpiece is currently around $1,800, plus additional fees for maintenance and styling. It's not cheap, but it does cost considerably less than hair transplants, which run anywhere from $5,000 to $15,000. The Hair Club is not the only company to offer hair-replacement systems. It's a booming business, with numerous rivals offering their own high-tech versions of glue-, tape-, or clip-on hairpieces. One thing is clear from the testimonials: Hair loss is deeply traumatic for people of both sexes, and for some, hairpieces provide welcome relief.

DOES BALDNESS REALLY MATTER TO WOMEN?

In July 2005, Great Britain's Committee of Advertising Practice passed a rule that would appear to validate the widely held belief that baldness is unattractive to women. As reported in the *Times* of London, "Drinks companies have been ordered to hire paunchy, balding men for advertisements to meet new rules forbidding any link between women's drinking and sex." The committee rejected an advertisement from Lambrini, a sparkling drink, because it featured a slim young man being "hooked" by three sexy babes at a fairground. "We would advise that the man in the picture should be unattractive—overweight, middle-aged, balding etc." instructed the committee.

"We're not sure they're qualified to decide for the nation who's sexy and who's not," responded Lambrini owner John Halewood, who noted that the ruling insulted a large portion of the male population and ignored the allure of stars such as Sean Connery and Bruce Willis. Lambrini reshot the ad with a man who was bald, but not overweight.

So who's right? Must you be Patrick Stewart to retain sex appeal once your hair begins to thin? The conventional wisdom is that women don't mind baldness as much as men think they do. Few studies have been done to determine the truth of this, but *Psychology Today* did sponsor such a survey in 1993. Fifteen hundred readers (64 percent of them women) were asked to complete questionnaires about the attractiveness of the opposite sex. The average age of the women was 34; the men, 37. "Women were relatively unconcerned about hair loss," reported the researchers. "Of those whose partner had a full head of hair, only 13 percent would be 'very upset' and 24 percent 'somewhat upset' at the prospect of his hair thinning. A mere 18 percent of women whose partners had already lost some hair acknowledged being very or somewhat upset." The women may simply have been resigned to the reality of their partner's thinning hair, but the numbers are nonetheless encouraging.

Fifty-two percent of the men surveyed believed women would agree with the statement, "I generally find bald men unattractive." Only 40 percent of women actually did agree. Some women thought bald men were cute, especially if they were already emotionally attached to the man.

Another survey, conducted in Australia, also sought to discover how women feel about men's hair. Psychiatrist Raj Persaud, investigating that study, offered some insight all men might do well to consider: "Your view of baldness is influenced by your own personal experience of people who are bald. As you get older your friends and acquaintances age with you, which means that older people tend to know more bald people. That may explain why in comparison with younger women, older women view baldness as a positive sign, suggesting maturity, knowledgeability and intelligence. Psychologists have also found that older women perceive younger balding men as more intelligent, successful, and likeable than nonbalding younger men. . . . The implication if you are a younger balding man is clear; you are likely to be found more attractive than nonbalding men your own age by slightly older women, so if you are after a date, these are the women to target." *Target* is an unfortunate choice of words, but the overall message is both practical and optimistic. Midlife men: Date women your own age, and you can quit worrying so much about your hair.

WILL I GO BALD? IF SO, WHEN?

If you've been blaming your mom for your hair loss, you're entitled. Researchers at the University of Bonn have confirmed that, in many cases, hair loss is genetically transmitted through the mother's side of the family. They studied ninety-five families in which two or more brothers were balding and found that a variant of the androgen-receptor gene was common to many of the brothers. The gene is on the X chromosome, which men get from their mothers. It increases the effects of androgens, which include testosterone and other male hormones. Androgens have long been known to cause baldness.

Although baldness on your mom's side of the family will largely determine whether you go bald, there are other factors as well. The hair loss of men on your dad's side may also be a predictor, to a lesser degree. Race plays a role too. Caucasian and Hispanic men are most likely to lose their hair, followed by African Americans and Asians. Native Americans and Eskimos are least likely to go bald.

What about women? About 10 to 15 percent of premenopausal women (age 50 and younger) experience some visible hair loss, and three out of four ladies over 65 have thinning hair. But because most women lose hair evenly all over their scalp and retain their frontal hairline, it's less conspicuous than in men. In fact, many women aren't aware of the loss at all until they notice their ponytail getting thinner.

The younger men are when they start to lose hair, the more extensive the loss is likely to be. The process typically begins in the twenties to early thirties. Half of all men will experience some baldness, either the male-pattern variety (the horseshoe of hair around the sides of the head), or temporal hair loss, where the frontal hairline recedes in an M shape.

Before you reach for the Propecia or Rogaine, you should know that a few other conditions may cause excessive hair loss. These include stress from illness or surgery, hormonal imbalance, and an over- or underactive thyroid gland. Hair loss due to stress or illness is usually temporary, and medication can treat the loss caused by hormone or thyroid imbalance. (See page 107 for more information about the thyroid.) However, Mother Nature is nothing if not evenhanded. As she removes hair from your head, she generously increases it in your ears and nose.

WHY DO SOME MIDLIFE GUYS SPROUT HAIR IN THEIR EARS AND NOSE?

There is no definitive answer, but the (relatively few) researchers interested in the question agree that it probably has to do with hormonal shifts. One theory is that changing hormones trigger a transformation in the hair follicles in your ears and nose. Where the follicles once produced fine, tiny hairs, they now produce longer, coarser hairs. It's the reverse of what happens on your head, where follicles that once produced actual hair now produce invisible fuzz. As for what causes the hormones to shift as men age, or why some hair follicles change and others don't, no one knows. It's a very common and benign condition, so little research money is devoted to studying it. A lot more R&D has gone into designing stylish nose-hair trimmers.

 THE GOOD NEWS ─────────────────

Welcome to the Man Spa

Just as millions of fiftyish men are beginning to sprout hair in all the wrong places, millions of twentyish men are deciding that they want some of the personal pampering women have enjoyed for decades. Male salons are cropping up all across America, places where guys can get "groomed," "camouflaged," and "hand-detailed" without hearing the words *pluck, dye,* or *manicure.* Eyebrow maintenance is what first pulls many men into salons such as American Male, Sport Clips, and Roosters Men's Grooming Centers, all of which have numerous franchises. The man spas, as they are sometimes called, are heavy on sports decor and feature amenities such as leather furnishings, men's magazines, big-screen TVs, free shoeshines, and complimentary beer.

Once a man has been lured inside (or pushed by his woman), he may avail himself of an array of personal grooming services, including facials; hairstyling and coloring; massage; manicures and pedicures ("hand and foot detailing"); eyebrow, chest, and back waxing; and paraffin dips for hands. You won't smell nail polish or flowery lotions, just the bracing aroma of beer and aftershave with perhaps a whiff of citrus—very James Bond, and very good news for men who are ready to turn their lonely personal grooming routine into a guilty pleasure.

WHAT ARE THE PROS AND CONS OF PROPECIA?

Propecia and the newer Proscar are brand names for the medication finasteride. The only difference between them is the dosage: Propecia is 1 milligram of finasteride, Proscar is 5. Because Propecia is expensive, some men buy Proscar and cut the pills into smaller doses—not recommended. Proscar is prescribed to treat prostate enlargement, not hair loss.

Finasteride works by blocking the conversion of testosterone into dihydrotestosterone, or DHT. High DHT levels are associated with baldness, so by preventing testosterone from converting into DHT, finasteride allows hair follicles that have become inactive to produce hairs again. In two twenty-four-month studies of men age 18 to 41, finasteride was shown to be fairly successful in treating hair loss. About 80 percent of the men studied maintained their base hair count, and 66 percent grew new hair. It usually takes about twelve months to see results from finasteride.

There are possible side effects with this drug, the most famous being loss of libido. The irony is obvious, as most men are concerned about hair loss because they fear it makes them less attractive. (Propecia cannot be taken by women, and pregnant women shouldn't even touch the pills, because doing so may cause birth defects.) The Propecia Web site has a patient product information page that lists sexual side effects, including "less desire for sex, difficulty in achieving an erection; and, a decrease in the amount of semen." The site goes on to say, "Each of these side effects occurred in less than 2% of men. These side effects went away in men who stopped taking PROPECIA. They also disappeared in most men who continued taking PROPECIA."

That reassurance was enough to persuade millions of men to take Propecia. Not all of them are convinced the side effects are rare or temporary. Their comments can be read on a number of forums, including propeciasideffects.com and askapatient.com. In February 2006, 87 men on askapatient .com described their experiences with the drug. Nearly all concluded that it grows hair superbly, but 35 of the men reported loss of sexual desire. Fifteen reported a change in their semen or erectile function, 11 reported testicular pain, and 9 reported breast enlargement. A few complained that their penis had developed a curvature. Their anguish comes through loud and clear. Wrote one man, "From looking at these forums, the 98% no side effects is a big lie. It annoys me that the FDA would approve something so destructive to our bodies." Another offered, "As far as preventing hair loss it worked like a charm. But now I've stopped taking it for almost a year, a lot of hair has fallen out (although it turns out it still looks fine overall), but I've got little man boobs THAT WON'T GO AWAY. I'm embarrassed to take my shirt off in public. Anyone up for suing Merck?"

Perhaps most disturbing, 22 of the 87 men reported experiencing depression, anxiety, and panic attacks while taking Propecia. Merck's site mentions nothing at all about these side effects. "I experienced my first panic attack that lasted for hours," reported one user. "Since then I have had horrible anxiety, shortness of breath, shaking, mood swings, and loss of appetite. It did not occur to me that Propecia may be causing these problems because Propecia's web site does not list these side effects. Thanks Propecia." Several men also claimed that Propecia made it more difficult for them to concentrate. Others lamented that the side effects did not decrease after they stopped taking the drug.

However, some men were ecstatic about the results. Some had *increased* sexual capacity with no side effects whatsoever. A man who had been on Propecia for eight months declared, "The negative experiences people have written about on this site astound me. . . . I have had great success with Propecia and now enjoy a thicker head of hair than I've had in the last two years. More than anything, it has greatly soothed my anxiety about losing my hair and allowed me to focus on the important things in my life."

These online forums are not scientific surveys, to be sure. But if you are contemplating taking Propecia, it would be worth your while to look through the comments. You could get lucky and enjoy years of thick hair, or you could end up like the tormented soul who wrote, "I used this shit for 11 months and now, 28 months later I still have side effects. I wonder if I'll ever get to normal. . . . I wish I could go back in time just to shave my head and avoid this poison."

WHAT IS MINOXIDIL?

Minoxidil (brand names Rogaine and Ronaxidil) is a slightly oily topical treatment for hair loss. It was originally developed as an oral or intravenous medication to treat high blood pressure, but at some point people noticed that it also caused hair growth in patients who were balding. No one knows exactly how it does this. The most popular theory is that it causes blood vessels in the scalp to dilate, increasing the hair follicles' exposure to blood flow and thereby spurring growth.

Minoxidil comes in strengths of 2 or 5 percent. The 5 percent solution gets better results, but women are warned that it may cause hair to grow on the sides of their face. Application is simple: You rub about twenty drops of minoxidil into your clean, dry scalp twice a day on the area you want to treat. Using more of the product will not yield better results.

The smaller the area you are treating and the more recent your hair loss, the better your results are likely to be. (It works best on the crown of the head.) A study of three hundred men over a forty-eight-week period found that 44 percent regrow hair. Those with the best results had been losing their hair for less than ten years, had a balding area that was less than four inches across, and had more hairs in the center of the balding area than men with poorer results.

If minoxidil works for you, the first hairs that grow will be peach-fuzzy and colorless. Eventually, after four months or longer, the new hair will look like your regular hair. It may take eight months for men to see complete results, and twelve months for women. One snag with the drug is that, as soon as you stop taking it, the new hair will stop growing. It will shed, eventually revealing your true pate.

Minoxidil has few side effects, and those are minor. Over a seven-year period, askapatient.com's minoxidil page had only 21 user comments. Complaints included itchy scalp, dandruff, and a few reports of heart palpitations. Clinical trials of the drug resulted in 6 percent of participants having an itchy scalp where the product was applied; using a dandruff shampoo can help alleviate the itchiness. Other possible side effects include burning, stinging, or redness when minoxidil is first applied to the skin. Be careful not to use it if your scalp is sunburned, irritated, or has any abrasions—the medication could be absorbed into your body and cause more serious side effects.

Dr. Peter H. Proctor, a pharmacologist and hair-loss expert, notes that "Minoxidil itself seems to have a relatively low order of side effects even when taken orally. There are reports of people surviving huge gram amounts taken in suicide attempts." (Note to men: When suicidally distraught over hair loss, don't bother to drink your Rogaine.)

THE GOOD NEWS ───────────────────

Hair Transplants Grow Up

In 2005, more than eighty thousand Americans paid between three and ten dollars per graft to have thousands of hair follicles transferred from the back of their heads to a more worthy location. The technique of hair transplantation has become so sophisticated that, for those who can afford it, it's hard to resist.

The success of hair transplantation is due to the phenomenon of *donor dominance,* first discovered in Japan in 1939 by a Dr. Oduka, who was looking for ways to repair scarred eyebrows and eyelashes. Donor dominance means that a hair follicle will retain its characteristics no matter where on the scalp (or body) it is placed. Follicles on the back of the head are generally predisposed to keep producing hairs throughout a lifetime, and if such a follicle is moved to another part of the head, it will maintain that characteristic. Hair transplants, therefore, solve the balding problem permanently.

Until the late 1980s, transplants involved grafting rows of round plugs containing fifteen to twenty-five hairs each onto the balding area. The effect screamed "doll's head." The state of the art has evolved dramatically since then. Now the best doctors use follicle-unit micrografts that contain one to four hairs. Single-hair micrografts are used at the front of the hairline to create a remarkably natural look, depending on the skill of the doctor.

Treating male-pattern baldness (men make up more

than 95 percent of hair-transplant patients) is as much a matter of artistry as technical skill. For that reason, it is crucial to vet your doctor very carefully before the procedure. In general, the less contrast between the skin and the hair, the easier it is to achieve a natural look. For instance, brown-haired, dark-skinned people and light-skinned blonds make good candidates. Light-skinned, dark-haired people can achieve excellent results, but there is less room for error because the mistakes show up more clearly on them. Curly hair achieves better coverage than straight, and coarse hair requires fewer grafts.

It is possible, but not easy, to repair a botched hair transplant. The field is extremely competitive, so it's worth your while to shop around for a doctor who has lots of before-and-after photos and satisfied patients whom you can call. Price shouldn't be your only guide—the most expensive doctor isn't necessarily the most talented.

WILL CERTAIN PRODUCTS OR HAIRSTYLES MAKE MY HAIR FALL OUT FASTER?

Yes. The key to hair preservation is to pamper the scalp from which your hair sprouts. Hairstyles that pull the hair, such as cornrows, ponytails, or tight buns, can scar the scalp and cause a type of permanent hair loss called *traction alopecia*. Tight hair rollers can do the same thing. Harsh products such as acidic (as opposed to alkaline) hair relaxers and hot oil treatments can cause the hair follicle to become inflamed, which can result in scarring and permanent hair loss. To prevent damaging your hair, experts warn against using more than one chemical product at a time. For example, do not use both a relaxer and a permanent color. If you must use both, choose a semipermanent color, which has no ammonia and less peroxide than the permanent type.

 ODD ARCHIVES

[Anthony Morrocco] calls his styles "lunar cuts," because they are done according to the moon's phases. Morrocco likens his approach to gardening: Hair is a crop, and the yield will be more bountiful if pruned carefully and harvested at just the right time. . . . He contends that cutting hair during the waxing of the moon makes it grow and that a haircut when the moon is waning retards growth.

—People Weekly, July 1987

CAN DYEING MY HAIR CAUSE CANCER? ARE "NATURAL" HAIR DYES SAFER THAN OTHERS?

For decades, there have been persistent rumors that coloring one's hair may cause cancer. In the 1990s, several large studies were conducted to address the concerns. One study of 573,000 women, sponsored by the FDA and the American Cancer Society in 1994, found that constant, prolonged (twenty years or more) use of black hair dye might slightly increase the risk of Hodgkin's lymphoma and multiple myeloma. The same year, another study of 99,000 women disputed that finding. In May 2005, the *Journal of the American Medical Association* published more recent findings that concluded there is no strong evidence of increased cancer risk among women who dye their hair. Currently, the FDA's official position is that there is no increased risk, and that the studies of black hair dye and certain cancers contradict one another.

If you're still concerned, using a semipermanent hair color should quell your fears. Semipermanent color coats the hair shaft but does not penetrate it, eliminating the supposed risk of a chemical entering the shaft and seeping into the scalp. Natural hair colors aren't much different than semipermanents, but some (not all) of them have no p-phenylenediamine (PPD), the chemical that has been cited as a possible cause of cancer. The natural hair colors are vegetable based, and some are free of peroxide and ammonia, which don't pose a serious health risk but which may irritate the scalp.

 EXPERT INPUT

Vanessa Vargas, Makeover Specialist

For more than a decade, Vanessa Vargas has honed her skills as an image consultant and hairstylist. At The Image

Studios in Chicago, Mrs. Vargas specializes in beauty makeovers for midlife women.

What are the mistakes middle-aged women often make in styling their hair?
Probably the biggest mistake is that they stick with what looked good on them when they were 22. Maybe they were coloring their hair a nice burgundy red that looked great with their skin at that time. As you age your skin changes, you may have broken capillaries, and being a redhead will bring out all those flaws in your skin.

How does the skin usually age? Does it get paler?
For everyone it's a little bit different. Someone who has fair skin may start to see a lot of pink in their skin, signs of rosacea. Women who are more of a yellow-based tone, like Hispanics, may see an almost green cast to the skin, an ashy look. They lose the golden tone they may have had at one time.

How do you remedy that?
It can be done with make-up. For yellow-based skin, they can go with a foundation that's yellow based and then use a bronzer. If you have fair skin, you want to be very careful with a bronzer, especially if you have pink in your skin, because you don't want to bring that out.

If women want a permanent fix, something a little bit more invasive, they can have facials and microdermabrasion, which definitely helps.

How does hair color relate to skin tone?

Stay away from unnatural tones in your hair across the board once you reach your midforties. If you want to be a redhead, you're going to be a natural tone of redhead, you're not going to be burgundy. As you get older, you always want to go lighter. Clients will say, "I was naturally a brunette." But you are not naturally a brunette anymore. You are naturally gray, and that's what you have to take into consideration.

What if you have to bleach your hair to go lighter, but it is more fragile or thinner than it used to be?

You never want the whole thing to go lighter. Let's say you were naturally a brunette. Your base could be a warm brown, and then you're going to do highlights on top of that. You won't be a solid blonde, because that would definitely be high maintenance and can damage the hair if you're 40 percent gray.

What about the other elements midlifers have to deal with, such as coarseness?

As you gray, the texture does change and turn more coarse. The styling tools you need to use are going to be very different than the ones you used when you were younger. The same goes for styling products. If your hair has become more coarse, you're going to want to use shampoos and styling aids that are moisturizing. You may want to use silicone-based shine when you style the hair.

What's been great in helping smooth out the hair is the flatiron, unless you have superfine hair. For everyone else, flatirons really help to seal the cuticle and give you that silky look.

How often do you have to use a flatiron?
It depends on your hair texture. I usually encourage my clients to shampoo every other day, not every single day, so if you use a flatiron today to style your hair, tomorrow you should be good to go. Maybe you'll need to touch up around your hairline, but you shouldn't have to go over the whole thing again.

Any other tools we should know about?
When you're younger, it's easier to wash and go. Although it's great to have a style that's easy to maintain, and you shouldn't have to spend an hour on your hair, you *are* going to spend a little more time than you did in your twenties. It can become curlier, it can become straighter, so you definitely want to take the time to round-brush it if you want to create volume.

What are some of your favorite styles or techniques for midlife women?
They should go shorter, but that's different for everyone. If you've had hair down your back all your life, then maybe top of the shoulders is as short as you'll want to go. For others it can be really short, a pixie cut, something fun. Hair now is being worn not so perfect. A little messy is OK.

When I first see middle-aged women, I can often tell what the best time in their life was, because they'll have that hairstyle forever. That ages them a whole lot. They'll say, "Well, it just works for me." I understand that it's easy, but I can find another cut that's equally easy and a little trendier.

Why do women keep these decades-old hairstyles?
When women keep their same cut throughout the years, it could be that it was really simple for them to style, or they really got it down. I even have clients who will say about a cut I did last year, "Please don't change it on me!" because they've got the technique down now. And I'll say, "You've got to keep moving. You can't stay stuck." So it's something that was easy, maybe something that they got tons of compliments on back then, and they got stuck there.

In terms of very short cuts, don't you need the right face and cheekbones to carry it off?
You do, which is why, even though you may be 40-plus, it doesn't mean you're going to go super short. It could be chin length, it could be bottom of the neck, top of the shoulders, but you do want to go shorter. When you get older, even in your late thirties, having hair past your shoulders is really going to weigh you down—unless you have a great look going for you, like Demi Moore. Most of the time, long hair ages you. You want to keep it light around the face.

What do you do when a person comes in with a big head of naturally curly hair and that person just isn't going to be flatironing it out?

We show her how to work with her natural curl. The biggest mistake women make is that they're afraid of product. When we go over product and show them how much should be used, they'll say, *"That* much?" For the most part, if your hair is even touching your shoulders, you need to use an amount of mousse the size of a lemon.

Here's how I tell my clients to style their hair. When it's dripping wet, comb it out and squeeze out the excess moisture. Put a lemon-sized squirt of mousse into your hand, squeeze some silicone shine into it, and stir it up. You don't want to use too much shine unless you have a lot of hair. For the average person, use one full squirt. Put the product in your hair, and *that is it.* Don't run your fingers through your hair later or tousle it. Just let it air dry, or use a diffuser. Lots of women think they can play with it all day. Not if you have curly hair.

Doesn't all that product make your hair stiff?

If you use a mousse, your hair should not get hard and stiff. Usually you find that problem with gel. What also helps break down that stiff feeling is mixing in the silicone shine.

Any other suggestions?

Women tend to be afraid to follow trends when they reach a certain age. I'll advise them to take little bits and pieces of whatever the trend may be and make it their own. For example, bobs are really in right now, so you can customize a bob. If you want a simple cut but want to make it a little trendier, you could do a heavy side bang. To stay current and look well put-together and polished, you do need to follow the trends on some level.

IS IT SAFE TO DYE MY PUBIC HAIR?

More traumatic than the first gray hair on your head, the first gray pubic hair feels like your personal ticket to Grannyville. You can pluck it—painful—or you can trim the whole area and minimize the effect. Or, if the gray hairs start to vastly outnumber the others, you can dye it. The experts at Columbia University Health Services' Web site, goaskalice.com, recommend against this practice because hair products are tested on scalps, not the pubic area, so there is no way to guarantee their safety. However, these experts also realize that people who want to dye their pubic hair are going to do it regardless of the risk, so they offer the following advice:

- Choose the least abrasive type of product, one that is semipermanent as opposed to permanent. If your goal is to cover gray, this shouldn't pose a problem, because permanent dyes are only necessary if you want to lighten hair. Semipermanent color will gradually fade over four to six weeks.

- Since pubic hair is more dense and coarse than the hair on your head, thicker products, such as gels and creams, are the best choice when dying the pubic area. In addition to providing better coverage, they are less likely to drip. Products intended for men's beards are a good choice.
- Use a skin-patch test first. Hair color may cause an allergic reaction or irritation, including burns, itching, redness, blisters, or hair loss. Follow the skin-patch directions that come with the product, and wait at least forty-eight hours to make sure you don't have a reaction.
- Protect the genital area. Color only the hair that covers the pubic bone. Don't get the chemicals anywhere near your genitals, as the dye can cause extreme irritation to sensitive skin and mucous membranes, even if it caused no harm to your arm during the skin-patch test. For extra protection, cover the genital area with petroleum jelly before you apply the product. You can also put a washcloth over your genitals when you're applying the dye and while washing it off.

MY EYEBROWS ARE FADING AWAY. WHAT CAN HELP?

Many women notice their eyebrows becoming thinner and grayer as years go by. If you were a heavy plucker in your youth, the problem may be exacerbated, because many of those plucked hairs will never grow back. The wrong type of eyebrow can certainly add years to your face. The worst offenders are brows that are too close together, penciled in too darkly, too thin, unkempt, or the wrong shape. There are quite a few options for improving your brows, some much more sensible and effective than others.

Brow pencil (or powder) is the choice of most women. The problem is, it can be difficult to make it look natural unless you have a fairly well-defined brow in the first place. Professional brow artists can help by shaping your brow to flatter your bone structure. They may also provide you with a template of the correct brow shape for you to follow at home. Good luck with that, unless you were an art major. With patience and a steady hand, you may eventually master the technique. Touch-ups at the salon can keep you on track.

Gray eyebrow hairs are especially frustrating: Pluck them, and you've lost another precious hair; leave them in, and you see Jane Goodall when you look in the mirror. Tinted eyebrow gel can help, or you can get your brows professionally colored at a salon. Do not use hair color products on your brows; they may damage your eyes.

Eyebrow tattoos never really caught on, with good reason. They're scary, unnatural looking, and permanent. In addition, as time passes the pigment may take on a bluish hue. The tattoo can be removed by laser, but then the brow will be entirely hairless. Don't risk it. If you're tempted, try some of the temporary brow tattoos that can be purchased online.

False eyebrows are an option for people whose brows are extremely thin and who don't want to have eyebrow transplant surgery (see below). The brows are made of human or synthetic hair and were developed for people with alopecia (total lack of body hair) or who have a temporary hair loss due to disease or chemotherapy. The false brows come in three or four basic shades and one shape (different for men and women), which you can bend to fit your natural brow line. They are attached with adhesive and can't be worn in water or at night.

Women or men who can't bear the sight of their thinning brows and have some expendable income might want to try eyebrow transplants. Plastic surgeons in the United States have been doing the procedure for many years to repair scarred brows. The results can be remarkably natural looking, but the work must be done by a very experienced and talented surgeon.

Typically, hairs from the scalp just behind and above the ear are harvested and transplanted to the brow, follicle by follicle, at exactly the right angle and density. The number of grafts per brow varies from about 75 to as many as 350, with men usually requiring more than women. Brow transplantation is performed in the doctor's office with local anesthesia. It takes about three to four hours, depending on how many assistants are helping the doctor. For a few days after the surgery there will be tiny scabs; when they fall off, the brow will look basically the same way it did before the surgery until the new hairs grow in. There is often some bruising around the eyes as well, which may last about a week. Most eyebrows are restored in either one or two sessions, with about eight months between sessions.

Because the grafts are taken from the scalp, the new brow hairs will grow long, just as they would if they had stayed in their original location. That means you'll need to trim them frequently, and the trimmed hairs won't have the same tapered look as natural brow hairs. There are aspects of the procedure that even the most gifted surgeon can't predict. For instance, the angle of the grafts may change as the wounds heal and contract, making the transplanted hairs stick up a little as opposed to lying flat. Is the surgery worth the imperfections? It's a personal choice, but it's nice to have the option.

 ODD ARCHIVES

Always on top of things, [hairdresser Maurice] Cohen, 40, has been zapping up to 50 people a week this summer with enough static electricity to make their hair stand on end. . . . The customer stands on a rubber stool, placing both hands on a steel globe that is actually a Van de Graaff generator. Then Cohen throws a switch and the sphere begins to hum, sending a harmless surge of static electricity through the customer's tingling arms and chest, into her scalp. . . . "You can be a punk for a night without having to stay that way," raves Jan Zemanek, 26.

—*People Weekly,* September 1984

HOW CAN I GET RID OF MY PEACH FUZZ?

By the time they reach 50, most women have made the acquaintance of Epilady, Tweezerman, or the many creams, lasers, and electronic torture devices designed to remove unsightly moustache and eyebrow hairs. Menopause, with its drop in estrogen, sometimes brings a new challenge: downy fuzz on the face. Although you may only notice it when looking in a magnifying mirror, you know from seeing other peach-fuzzed ladies that in the right light it glows like a halo. Foundation clings to it, making it look even heavier. The best way to deal with that is to go easy on the foundation, let it set, and then pat off any excess with a slightly damp sponge.

To reduce the peach fuzz, you might try the prescription cream Vaniqa, which works within the follicle to slow the growth of hair. The cream is applied twice a day, and according to the manufacturer you should see results in four to six weeks. It does not work for everyone, however. If nothing happens in six months, Vaniqa is not for you. Its makers claim that Vaniqa works best in combination with laser treatments, but laser doesn't work on light hair like peach fuzz. Right now, Vaniqa is the only FDA-approved topical medication formulated to treat facial hair in women. You will need to keep applying it in order to maintain the effect, but some doctors advise their patients to use it only every other day once their down has been reduced.

five

THE PAPERWORK

WHAT HAPPENS IF I DON'T HAVE A WILL?

A lot of what happens if you die without a will depends on who and what you leave behind. Most everyone has an unpleasant story about grasping relatives and their bad behavior at the time of a loved one's death, sometimes even loved ones who *had* a will. Since you won't be around to enjoy the show, you might not care if the "good" daughter is duking it out with the "prodigal" daughter over the dining-room chairs, each with her own convoluted rationalizations of why you would have wanted those chairs to go to *her*. The arguments seldom stop with two rivals but often spread through entire extended families like ripples on a pond of bile, creating bad feelings that last for years. If this image causes you pain rather than perverse pleasure, you should not die without a will.

Although most people have spent some time reflecting and mentally parceling out their worldly goods, at least 50 percent of Americans die intestate, that is, without a will. Every state has laws that govern what happens to your property if you die intestate, and they typically follow a logical pattern. Undesignated money and property usually will go to a surviving spouse. If there is no spouse, it will be divided among surviving children. If there are no children, it will go to other locatable family. If there is no family, the state gets the booty. Having the court decide the distribution of your goods is costly and time-consuming. The court costs are deducted from the assets, and if anyone in the family challenges the court's decision, the result may be a case that is tied up in red tape for years with little left for anyone by the time it labors to its conclusion.

Domestic partners should not assume that there is a common-law clause that will treat the surviving partner as a spouse. Those laws vary from state to state, and for same-sex partners, there are only three states that will honor your relationship with spousal status: Vermont, California, and Maine. All of them require you to register as a same-sex partnership in order to be able to inherit property. At the very least, check your state's inheritance and intestate laws if you don't have a will but do have a domestic partner.

There are problems beyond property disbursement that can arise if you don't have a will when you die. If you are responsible for minor children, a will is *the* document that names your chosen guardian for a minor child, as well as distributing any funds designated toward the raising of that child. The National Center on Grandparents Raising Grandchildren estimates that grandparents are raising 4.5 million children, about 6 percent of the population, and it is a growing trend. Most of the grandparents raising children are between the ages of 55 and 64. If you are among them, you need a will. No one wants children lost in the state system or going to live with chain-smoking Aunt Lola and her pack of wheezing Chihuahuas because a child's best interests were not legally documented.

Speaking of Chihuahuas, if you have pets, a will is likewise the place to make known what you would like to happen to them if you die before they do. Since we are past the age of the Vikings, when it was acceptable to sacrifice your animals and cross the Rainbow Bridge together, dying without a will might condemn beloved pets to spend their last days in a shelter. Although it is inappropriate to use your will to try to force a relative to keep your pets, you can designate resources for their proper placement.

Your will doesn't have to name every item you own, but it should cover your major assets and what you would like to happen to them after you are gone. A separate list for sentimental items you would like to give to specific individuals can be attached to the will. If you have no family or anyone whom you would like to inherit your money, you still may find it worthwhile to will your estate to a favorite charity rather than the state in which you live.

IS IT WISE TO WRITE A DO-IT-YOURSELF WILL?

You've watched too many old movies if your idea of a do-it-yourself will is a scratchy, handwritten document found in the attic just before all the family treasures are hauled away to Value Village. Scratchy, handwritten wills are valid in some states, but they're not recommended, because they usually leave out important information and are too vulnerable to being contested by cranky relatives who feel they are not getting their share.

However, there are many do-it-yourself wills that are perfectly acceptable, as long as they contain basic elements that make them less likely to end up in probate. (See "What is probate?" below.) Finding a template for a do-it-yourself will is easy. Two Web sites (of many) that offer fill-in-the-blank style wills are nolo.com and ilrg.com. The latter is the Internet Legal Research Group, and its downloadable forms are categorized by state to make sure that its legal documents conform to the appropriate laws. If you don't have Internet access, the local office-supply store often carries legal forms as well.

There are two items every will must include in order to avoid costly court battles. First, you must name an executor, that is, a person who will manage and carry out the directives of the will. Second, you must name beneficiaries, the persons who will inherit the property. It's a good idea to name at least two of each, so that if the first executor is dead or incapacitated, the other one can fulfill that function. Although it is not typical to include addresses and phone numbers in a will, an attached document with that information can be very helpful if you have not distributed copies of your will to the executor and beneficiaries. It is common sense to at least tell these folks where your will is located, so your family doesn't have to turn into a SWAT team, destroying your home looking for important papers.

Do-it-yourself wills are appropriate for anyone with simple assets, such as bank accounts, investments, a home, and cars. You must specify in your will how you would like these assets divided if there is more than one beneficiary.

Consulting a lawyer is wise if you own a business or assets in conjunction with people other than your spouse, if you need to set up trusts that will provide care for another person, or if you have complicated directions for how you want your property dispersed. Rather than pay a lawyer to write the entire document, you can request a consultation that focuses only on the portion of your will that needs clarification. Most states have legal aid societies whose lawyers donate a limited pro bono consultation that may be just what you need for your questions.

Many people don't realize that insurance policies or retirement accounts that have named beneficiaries will supersede the directives in your will. Remember all those benefits you signed up for when you started your job ages ago? Maybe the beneficiary was your first wife, and now you are on your third. If you die and your will says everything goes to "my darling wife, Heather," but Margaret the First was the beneficiary on one of those policies, guess what? Margaret will be collecting. It pays to have all these documents together and handy. It also pays to regard them as living documents, that is, documents that need to be reviewed and updated every few years. Life changes, and with multiple marriages and blended families being the norm these days, you need to maintain an updated will that is consistent with your other policies and accounts.

Regardless of whether you have a do-it-yourself will or a will constructed by a lawyer, make sure it is legal. Every state requires that your will be signed in front of at least two witnesses who have no interest in the will, and the witnesses must sign as well. Some states require three witnesses, and most require that the will be notarized. If your will is of the scratchy, handwritten variety, the entire document must be written in your handwriting to be legal.

 ODD ARCHIVES

Law will be simplified [over the next century]. Lawyers will have diminished, and their fees will have been vastly curtailed.

—Julius Henry Browne, journalist, 1893.

WHAT IS PROBATE?

Probate is the legal process by which your will is validated and the assets dispersed. Your executor will file papers with the local probate court that will include copies of the will for validation, a list of your assets and debts, appraisals of any property, and a list of the inheritors. The court makes sure that any outstanding debts and taxes are paid. The executor is usually responsible for carrying out these financial matters and making sure that the property is dispersed according to your wishes. If there is no executor, the court will appoint an administrator. Probate can be quite pricey, and all court and lawyer fees are deducted from the estate. Typically, the cost ends up being about 5 percent of the estate. That may not sound like much, but if part of your estate is your home, and that home is worth $300,000, that's a starting fee of $15,000, not counting the rest of your assets. Probate can drag on for months, depriving your beneficiaries of resources they may need in the meantime.

Probate laws vary from state to state. If your estate's worth is small enough, you may not have to go through probate. Each state has an upper limit of worth that defines whether you will need to go through the process. There are also certain assets, such as 401(k)s or insurance policies, that may fall outside of assets considered in probate, so your overall worth may be less once you deduct them. Still, avoiding probate altogether may be difficult.

One way to reduce the overall impact is to avoid costly lawyers' fees by having the executor of the will go through the process without an attorney. Because the laws are written in a convoluted, cryptic fashion, they may be daunting to an ordinary person. But most probate is clerical in nature—certain papers have to be filed in a timely manner and the executor needs to show up to the court dates. With the assistance of a good self help book or a local law library, it can be done. The executor will have to assess how difficult and time-consuming the process will be and how angry the heirs will be if a sizable portion of their inheritance lands in the coffers of the local law firm. Many financial advisors boldly state that probate does nothing more than add unneeded expense and that it can and should be avoided at all costs.

You can also reduce the size of your estate by gifting money and putting property in other people's names. Reducing the size of your estate will reduce probate fees. However, the only sure-fire way to avoid probate is to establish a living trust, discussed below.

WHAT IS A LIVING TRUST?

A living trust is a legal document that allows you to transfer assets to beneficiaries in a way that avoids probate and estate-settlement costs. A living trust and a living will are two entirely different documents with different purposes and should not be confused. Living wills are explained on page 164.

The operative word in "living trust" is *living*. This is a trust established by you, while you are alive. Essentially, you transfer any or all of your assets into a trust, with yourself as the trustee and the beneficiary. You can add cash or titles or property to the trust at any time. As trustee, you have control over the assets and can use them as you wish. You can set up how they are to be used in your declining years and you can designate how they are to be used and distributed after your death. As part of the process of setting up a living trust, you name a successor trustee who will manage the trust if you become mentally or physically unable to do so yourself, and after you die.

Living trusts come in two varieties: revocable and nonrevocable. A revocable trust can be changed at any time, whereas a nonrevocable trust must stay as it was set up, regardless of any changing circumstances. Most people choose the revocable type for the flexibility.

People typically set up living trusts because they want to avoid probate. However, depending upon the state you live in, you might want to do some research before you make a decision. Some states have changed their laws to make probate faster and cheaper. Although probate does tend to drag on, the court supervision provides more legal protection if your wishes are complex—some succeeding trustees have been less than honest in their distribution of living-trust assets. A living trust does not exempt you from estate taxes, income taxes, or debts, so it should not be viewed as a money-saving device, other than the money it may save you by avoiding probate.

The advantages of a living trust, in addition to sparing your heirs the cost and waiting period of probate, include financial protection for you as you age and may not be able to manage your money, and financial protection for minor children or children who may require care after you are gone (such as adult children with physical or mental disabilities). If you decide to go the living trust route, be aware that your planning should still include a living will, a power of attorney, and a regular will for assets that are not in the trust.

Living trusts have gotten a lot of attention lately, and consumers have been bombarded with solicitations from businesses trying to sell the trusts. Unscrupulous salespeople often use fear tactics or try to hard-sell consumers other financial products once they've obtained their personal information. If these salespeople call you about "special offers" on their living trusts or try to make an appointment at your home, don't get taken in. You can always call the consumer protection department of the state bar association, or the Better Business Bureau, to check out the company that is making these offers, but it is best if *you* are the one investigating whether a living trust is right for you. Living trusts are usually prepared by an attorney, financial planner, or insurance agent. Your family, friends, or colleagues should be able to steer you toward someone they consider trustworthy.

WHAT IS A LIVING WILL?

A living will is the document that directs the type of health care you wish to receive at the end of your life or if you become incapacitated and cannot communicate. Most of us have made heroic statements such as, "I don't want to be kept alive by artificial means," when we are perfectly healthy and death seems far away. But it is quite a different experience to sit down and commit those thoughts to a legal document and to detail the particulars, as you must do when you write a living will. Not only are you confronted with your own mortality, but you must actually imagine yourself helpless and in pain, with your body attached to various tubes and needles. If you are fortunate enough to have reached the age of 50 without knowing anyone who has faced a terminal illness, it may be very difficult to picture yourself in that condition. If, on the other hand, you have experienced the death of a loved one, the memory may be too painful to revisit. Even people in between these two extremes are often quite happy to put off writing a living will indefinitely. That leaves no one who really wants to do the deed, but everyone past the age of 50 ought to.

As a responsible adult, you need to make life-and-death decisions ahead of time so that they don't fall to your family or the health-care system. Even if you have told your family that you do not wish to be kept alive via medical technology, without a legal document it is difficult to prove your wishes in court, and that is where your family may end up. Without a living will, every effort will be made to keep you alive. Today's medicine is so sophisticated that "keeping you alive" can translate into prolonging death for interminable periods of time, with no hope of restoring any kind of normal function. All of us are aware of such cases, and most of us don't want to be one.

Living-will templates are available from many do-it-yourself Web sites, and often your health-care provider has them as well. They are sometimes referred to as health-care declarations or advance directives. Make sure the template, or any document you create from scratch, does not lapse into vague language such as, "No extraordinary care is to be taken if my situation is hopeless and irreversible." What, exactly, do those words mean? Extraordinary care or heroic measures to one person might include a feeding tube or a tracheotomy tube, while for another such interventions might be routine. Instead of saying "no extraordinary care," make sure that your living will states clearly what you want if your situation appears terminal: water but not food, water and food, oxygen but not a ventilator. If you want everything that is medically possible done, even if you are reduced to the status of a gherkin for the next twenty years, make that clear as well.

As for "hopeless and irreversible" conditions, it is often hard for doctors to predict what will meet that criteria. In your living will, you should clearly state a timeline when heroic measures are to be withdrawn. Most people are willing to endure uncomfortable medical treatment if they believe their function will be restored. But if heroic efforts have not been successful, your family and physicians need to know when it is OK to terminate treatment. Naturally, if you are cognizant and in your right mind, you can direct your own health care and state what you will and will not endure. The living will is only invoked if you are not able to communicate. If you don't have one, take a deep breath, draw one up, attach it to your regular will, give a copy to your primary physician and to your power of attorney (see below), and then get on with your delusions of immortality.

WHAT IS POWER OF ATTORNEY?

A power of attorney is a document that designates a specific agent to make decisions for you either immediately or if you become incompetent. A durable power of attorney becomes active when it is signed and is very sweeping in its powers, allowing the agent to make all kinds of decisions for you, the principal. The agent is allowed to sign documents for you, handle your finances, and speak on your behalf. Medical and financial powers of attorney are limited to those areas, and they will not become active until your doctor writes a letter stating that you are no longer able to make competent decisions. If you would like your competency to be determined by two independent doctors (you may be more comfortable having a second opinion), you can write that into your document.

All powers of attorney will stay in effect until you revoke them, until a predetermined date is reached, until you become competent again, or until you die. The forms for power of attorney are fairly standard and can be found on Web sites offering do-it-yourself wills, at your doctor's office, or at the local office-supply store. Some states require that they be notarized and/or witnessed, so you'll want to check on that.

Revoking a power of attorney is a simple matter of filling out a power of attorney revocation form and presenting it the next time a decision needs to be made that your designated agent might be involved in. You don't even need to be competent in order to revoke your power of attorney. The salient feature of a power of attorney is that it is completely voluntary and the principal's choice. Whether or not the principal is bats is of little consequence if she wants to revoke her power of attorney. Situations like this can be very frustrating to other family members when a power of attorney is truly needed and the principal doesn't quite see it that way.

There are limitations on power of attorney to ensure that the principal is not abused. For example, your agent cannot force you to accept medical treatment that you don't want. Even if it would be in your best interest to receive a particular medical intervention, and you are completely out of your mind, if you start screaming when they come with the big needle, your agent cannot sit on you and say, "Go ahead and stick him, boys!" That's a no-no.

The agent also cannot have you committed to a mental institution, have you undergo psychiatric surgery (lobotomy) or receive electroconvulsive therapy, or force you to have an abortion. He or she can withhold medical or comfort care from you only if that authority is specified in your living will. It is frightening to imagine the scenarios that led to these safeguards. To avoid potentially abusive situations with ex-spouses, a power of attorney naming a spouse as agent is automatically terminated after a divorce. There are also laws in place to protect the person who has power of attorney: He or she is not legally liable for any of your bills or for medical decisions that are carried out in good faith and in accordance with your wishes.

A good reason to designate powers of attorney sooner rather than later is the enactment of the Health Insurance Portability and Accountability Act of 1996 (HIPAA). HIPAA laws forbid health-care providers and banks to share any information about you without a signed release. When you go to a doctor's office or hospital for the first time, you are required to sign a HIPAA release form. But if you're suddenly incapacitated by a stroke or an accident, you may not be able to sign the forms. If you have not designated a power of attorney, it may be very difficult for anyone—even your spouse or adult child—to get access to your condition, to be consulted on medical decisions, or to be able to pay a bill for you (unless the person is a cosigner with you on a bank account).

People often don't realize that a power of attorney becomes obsolete when you die. Because it is a document of choice, your agent is no longer allowed to make decisions for you once you are no longer around. If you don't have a valid will naming an executor, the immediate decisions, such as what to do with your body, will be assigned to the next of kin, assuming a next of kin can be found. You can, of course, name the same agent as your executor, but to ensure continuity of your wishes, it is helpful to have both a will and a power of attorney.

WHAT IS DISABILITY INSURANCE, AND WHO NEEDS IT?

The purpose of disability insurance is to provide you with a percentage of your wages if you become disabled and cannot work, either permanently or for a period of time while you rehabilitate. Most policies provide between 45 and 65 percent of your current wages. Many employers provide disability insurance as a benefit, but if you are independently employed or your employer doesn't provide it, you might want to consider a policy, particularly if you work in a profession with a high risk for injury, such as construction or driving. In general, our risk for disease and injury increases as we age, and people over 45 are more vulnerable regardless of their profession.

The trick to choosing disability insurance has to do with how the policy defines *disability*. Reading the fine print is extremely important. Most policies will not pay unless your condition meets their definition of total disability. The best policies have what is called the *own occupation* definition of disability: You are considered totally disabled if you are too disabled to perform the duties of your regular occupation. With an own-occupation policy, if you can't work construction due to a back injury, you can work a telephone job and collect your disability benefit. Most people would prefer to work, and considering that the benefit only pays about half of your former wages, you may *need* to work. This type of policy is definitely the most generous in helping you to maintain your income.

Unfortunately, own-occupation policies are getting harder to find. The majority of policies are now called income-replacement insurance. Under an income-replacement policy, you are considered totally disabled only if you are not working in *any* occupation. If you get a little part-time job, good-bye claim. You might assume there is a huge disparity in premiums between these two types of policies, but often there is not. You just need to shop around and specifically ask for an own-occupation policy.

The worst type of policy to have, and the one that is most often provided by employers, is called a gainful-occupation policy. The reason that it is not to your advantage is that the insurance company gets to decide if you can actually work or not. If you become disabled to the point where you cannot perform your regular employment, the insurer can still deny your claim. They may rule that, although you cannot work construction any longer, you can certainly work at a telephone job. Even if you don't *have* a telephone job. The risk of spending long periods of time fighting the insurance company through endless submissions of proof of disability and actual litigation is fairly high with this type of policy. People with high-risk occupations might want to consider supplementing with another policy if this is the type your employer offers.

Gainful-occupation policies are modeled on the definitions of disability that Social Security uses in its eligibility determinations. If you don't have a private disability policy and you become disabled, you can always apply for Social Security Disability Insurance, even if you are under the age of 65. For people with a terminal condition, applying for SSDI is not difficult and is often a blessing. For everyone else, it can be a nightmare. Using the gainful-occupation definition of disability, Social Security turns down 70 percent of its applicants on the first try, ruling that the applicants can do *some* kind of work. They don't care if you were a rocket scientist and now you are blind. You can sell lightbulbs over the phone for minimum wage—that is work. It doesn't matter how great a wage loss you have incurred or that you have looked for months and there are no lightbulb jobs available in your area. The fact that you *can* work according to their definition is all that matters, not whether you *have* work.

SSDI should never be relied upon as a form of unemployment. Most people challenge their SSDI denial and endure reconsiderations and judicial appeals that can take up to three years to resolve. The good news is that 60 percent of applicants who go through the appeals process win their appeals and are entitled to benefits dating from the time they applied. The bad news is that disabled workers need an income *now,* not three years from now.

If you do apply for SSDI, remember that it is perfectly legal to collect disability from both Social Security and your private disability insurer. It would be your personal disability policy that might deny double-dipping, not Uncle Sam. The amount of monthly benefit in an SSDI claim is based on work credits—how much you worked in a given period of time and what your earnings were. At this time, the maximum monthly benefit for a single, disabled worker is about $900. The maximum for a disabled worker with a spouse and one or more children is about $1,600. If you are a high-wage earner, the 45 to 65 percent of a private policy may be more advantageous.

When choosing a personal disability policy, there are a few elements to scrutinize in addition to the definition of disability. You'll want to know about the benefit period (how long the policy will pay a monthly benefit), the elimination period (how long you must wait before you receive your first check after disability has been determined), and residual claims (a provision that allows you to still receive a benefit after you return to work due to lost wages or time). The fine print, personal risk, and cost will guide your decision.

WHAT IS LONG TERM CARE INSURANCE, AND WHO NEEDS IT?

Long term care insurance is a policy that provides for care, either at your home or in a facility, should you become disabled and require assistance in what is called your "activities of daily living"—for example, eating, dressing, bathing, or toileting. It differs from disability insurance in that it does not pay benefits based on your wages, nor is it related to your ability to work. Its purpose is to provide comprehensive care and to keep you in your home as long as possible, if that is where you want to be. Most people want desperately to stay in their own homes, even if they are gimping along rather slowly and have safety risks that make other members of the family very uncomfortable. Long term care insurance is one way to preserve the independence of living at home for as long as possible. It also gives you greater buying power if the time comes when you must enter a retirement facility and you want to go to Eden Glen rather than Medicaid Gulch.

There are arguments pro and con concerning the need for long term care insurance. Some think it is the latest fear-based scam to get you to buy a policy you don't need. The decision to purchase a long term care policy should be based on your age, health, and financial situation, not on an insurance agent's scaring you with visions of living your last days in a cardboard box in back of the Safeway. As of now, many people of the age to cash in on their long term care policies have not needed to, so they have not gotten their money's worth. Statistically, the majority of people haven't required long term care at the end of their lives, and stays in nursing homes have tended to be less than a year. If you are truly without resources, Medicaid *will* pay for your long term care, and you won't have to live in a box.

However, that picture may change for the baby-boom generation. Life expectancy is increasing, and by the time boomers are elderly, they will be living several years longer than the generation before them. More chronic conditions will be managed through advances in medicine. In short, it's becoming harder and harder to get rid of us. Since 80 percent of people over 65 manage one chronic condition, and those over 80 manage at least two, the odds of needing help are greater the longer we live. Anyone paying attention to public affairs has noticed that support for programs such as Medicare and Medicaid is becoming a financial nightmare. Who knows what those programs will look like in twenty years? Long term care facilities are already starting to limit or deny service to Medicaid clients. This is the new reality. While you need not be scared into buying insurance because of it, now might be a good time to weigh the options by taking a shrewd look at your resources and health risks.

The main factors guiding your decision will be your age, your savings and investments, and the amount you will realistically be able to save by retirement. If you are fiftyish and won't have many resources after retirement but will have too much to be eligible for public assistance, you might want to consider long term care insurance. If you own your own home and have considerable investments and savings, you may not need the policy because you can pay for your own care. Current long term care costs range between $30,000 and $150,000 annually, depending on the type of care and where you live. Those costs won't be going down.

A drawback to purchasing long term care insurance if you are of limited means is that you are stuck with the premium for the rest of your life or until you cash in the policy. Some people let their policies lapse after retirement because they simply can't pay the bill anymore, thus wasting a lot of money. A rule of thumb suggested by the industry: If your policy premium is more than 7 percent of your gross income, you can't afford the insurance.

Although you probably don't need to buy a policy until you are 50, the price jumps significantly after age 55, so there is a window of opportunity between the affordable and unaffordable. At 50, a policy will cost you roughly a hundred dollars per month; after 55, it will double and keep on going up the older you are. So premium cost will affect your decision on whether to buy a policy.

Finally, consider your health and your family-health history. If you already have a serious health condition, such as diabetes, you may not qualify for long term care insurance. (A health questionnaire and/or health screening is required when you apply.) No one has a crystal ball, but if your risk for chronic conditions is higher due to the presence of illnesses such as stroke, Parkinson's disease, diabetes, or dementia in close family members, you might want to consider a policy. The difference between those conditions and others such as heart attack or cancer is that the former typically result in years of slow decline requiring a lot of assistance. Most people prefer not to rely on their family to provide extensive care, because they hate the idea of becoming a burden. Providing for your own care is one way to preserve some dignity.

Be aware that all policies are not alike, and you must be a savvy consumer when inquiring about them. The cheapest policies only cover two years' worth of care, but most people won't need more than two years. It's a gamble, like anything else. The difference in price between a ten-year policy and a lifetime policy can be negligible, but the difference in the actual benefit may be huge. Some policies authorize only a certain number of hours of care per day, while others will pay you a daily rate regardless of the number of hours you use. This can be a great boon for those who are cash-poor. If your policy pays you $150 per day and you only use one hour of care, you can pocket the balance. Some policies will guarantee that your premium will only go up by a certain percent, and others will not. Policies usually will increase their benefit each year by a certain percentage to adjust for inflation in cost of care, but the amount will vary by policy.

There is always a chance that the policy you buy won't pay for all your care when you need it. You can combine your policy payout with your Social Security, savings, and pensions to pay for care, and with insurance at least you will have part of your care covered without draining all your resources. Again, you must scrutinize the details, ask a lot of questions, and review your own finances to make sure you are getting the biggest bang for the buck. Never let an agent bully you or try to instill fear. Buy only what seems reasonable for you and your situation.

WHO NEEDS LIFE INSURANCE?

The main purpose of life insurance is to pay a cash benefit to survivors when you die. Your premiums are based on how much you'd like that benefit to be. There are two main types of life insurance, *term* and *permanent*. Most people buy term insurance, which means you pay premiums on the policy for a given period of time, such as twenty years, and then the policy ends. Some term policies allow you to renew after the twenty-year period, at a progressively higher rate, but most won't let you do so after the age of 75.

People purchase term insurance for the death benefit only, and the premiums are relatively low.

Permanent insurance, also known as cash-value insurance, is a lifelong policy that allows you to borrow money against the cash value portion of the policy. The disadvantage is that you will have to pay the premiums forever or lose the policy, including the cash savings. However, permanent policies do give you the option of paying the premium out of the policy itself if you go through a financially tight period (if you do this, the overall benefit will go down). You can borrow money from your permanent policy to pay for your children's education, a down payment on a house, or for extra income without the hassle of qualifying for credit. You do have to repay the loan with interest, or the payout to beneficiaries will be significantly reduced or nonexistent. The premiums for permanent insurance are much higher than those for term—between five and ten times as much.

Life insurance is one of those things that is better to buy when you are young and have young children. The older you are, the more expensive it gets. If you have term insurance and want to renew it after the twenty- or thirty-year term is up, you may find the premiums have gone sky high due to your age. If your health is poor or you have any chronic conditions, it may be too expensive, or you may be flat-out rejected by insurers. If you smoke, if your weight is even modestly above "desirable" on the weight tables used by the insurance companies, or if you use alcohol, your rates can go up as much as 35 percent. Life insurance policies require a physical that includes a urine test that will pick up nicotine and other drugs.

Many people feel that it doesn't make sense to carry life insurance after the children are grown, which is why twenty-year term insurance is so popular. Life insurance is intended to protect your dependents from financial difficulties by replacing the income you would have earned had you not died. If your children are grown and supporting themselves and you are retired and living off your investments (or soon will be), there is no earned income to replace and less reason to carry life insurance.

However, not everyone's life moves along on so tidy a track. With people marrying later and today's high divorce rates, it's not unusual for couples in their forties to be starting their first or second families and requiring life insurance at an older age. For these folks and others who have been shut out of life insurance because of disability or higher risks, there are special-needs advocates who can help you find competitive life-insurance rates.

 EXPERT INPUT ——————————————————

Lewis Wallensky and Andrea Spatz, Financial Planners

As a certified financial planner (CFP), Lewis Wallensky has been guiding clients for forty years. He has taught financial planning at UCLA, lectured at Stanford University, and been named by *Medical Economics* magazine as one of the nation's top 150 financial planners. Andrea Spatz has been a CFP since 1993. Before joining Lewis M. Wallensky Associates, she was a vice president at Bank of America and Security Pacific Bank. Their Century City office serves clients of all income brackets.

What are the most common financial issues for midlifers?

Lewis Wallensky: Everyone's situation is unique, but the main issue for midlifers is to start thinking about the time when they will no longer be working. If you work for a corporation, it's very simple: They may have a mandatory retirement age, such as 60 or 65, when they'll tell you, "Bye-bye, it's been nice knowing you." If you're self-employed, it's a whole different ball game. You can continue working for as long as you want. People at midlife need to take stock of where their life is, what their family situation is, their health, their obligations, their goals, and ultimately what they want their money to do for them.

How do you help clients with that process?

LW: Most people look at their assets and try to project what their income is going to be. We create a table that shows what income will be coming in, and when, and what they may need it for. But more important, and this is almost like being a psychotherapist, we get people to focus on what they really want to do. I don't think people are as honest with their goals internally as they are when discussing them with someone else. They get so focused on the quantitative issues—the money—that they lose track of the qualitative. They ask, "Can I do it financially?" when they should also be asking, "What is it that I really want to do?"

Are your clients pretty accurate at predicting what they will want to do?
LW: We have found, with some exceptions, that most people do not do in retirement that which they did not do before retirement. By and large, you don't wake up one day and say, "I'm gonna learn how to shoot 80." You're just not going to do it. People who are playing a round of golf once a week before they retire may initially play two rounds a week, but that's about it. People who have never been involved in charity before are not going to suddenly sit on fifteen different charity boards.

The key is, you don't know how much income you're going to need in retirement until you're living it. So when clients who are about to retire come into this office, we'll take a look at their pension, the income generated from their assets, and their Social Security. Then we'll say, "Let's guesstimate what you're going to need, and a year from now come back, and we'll talk about it. Until then, we'll keep your investments fluid." That is, if they have enough assets to do that. Not everybody does.

What about those warnings we hear: "You must have a million dollars saved for retirement" or, "Your retirement income must equal 70 percent of your preretirement income."

LW: That is much too general. We have some clients who are living on little more than their Social Security because they spent most of their assets raising their families. They have some life insurance and some long term care, and they're protected. That's financial planning also. Not everyone who uses a financial planner is rich.

Those numbers you hear are meaningless. It's an individual thing. Everybody lives differently. Do you belong to a country club? Do you travel a lot? Are your kids in four different cities, and will you need to travel to see them? Do your kids have kids who have problems that you'll want to help out with? How many grandchildren do you have? Do you care? Do you have aging parents who will need your help? These are the personal things you have to take into consideration.

How do you feel about long term care insurance?

LW: There are only two kinds of people who probably do not need it: those who are extremely wealthy and can afford to pay for care on their own, and those who are not wealthy at all and will be relying on the state. Everyone else should get it. The time to buy it is generally in your late fifties or early sixties. [The most cost-effective time may be between the ages of 50 and 55; see page 175.]

One of the things I hear from people all the time is, "I'm not going to buy this insurance. If anything happens to me, I don't care, I'll get rid of myself." The reality of life is, if you're at the point where you're going to need nursing care, it's not your decision anymore. It's going to be the decision of your family, in many cases your children. Maybe you've got a 50-year-old child who's raising an 18-year-old son, and where's the money going to come from? You may never need nursing care, but if you do, it will be a financial burden on your family unless you have long term care insurance.

Which should come first, saving for retirement or saving for your child's college education?
Andrea Spatz: Definitely saving for retirement. They don't give out scholarships for retirement. To pay for college, you can borrow against your house, your kid can work his way through school, he can go to a junior college to save money, he may receive some financial aid. A lot of colleges are throwing scholarship and grant money at students. There are many ways to pay for an education, but there's no way to pay for your retirement except you.

What general advice do you have for midlifers?
AS: The same that I'd say to any age group: Live within your means. We see a cross section of clients, from people with government jobs earning forty thousand to fifty thousand dollars a year, to people with Hollywood jobs earning obscene amounts. It doesn't matter where they are on the spectrum, some people have trouble living within their means. If you can learn to live on less than you make and put some aside, you will always be able to manage. And

you'll be able to take advantage of the market and grow a nest egg.

People overestimate the pleasure they get out of buying stuff. We are such a consumer society; it's so hard for so many people *not* to buy a flat-screen TV, *not* to take the fabulous trip, *not* to give their kid the designer education at the fanciest school. But people have a lot of stress when their finances are a mess. There's a lot to be said for having the peace of mind you get when your financial house is in order—to be able to leave a job you hate, to be able to send your kid to a good school because you've made some sacrifices along the way.

Sometimes, when clients get an inheritance, we'll remind them, "This is it. There's not going to be anything else." And they'll go out and buy themselves a new car or redecorate the house. Then they're scrambling in their older age.

LW: A lot of people 50 and above are going to have a second phase of income. Most of them own a house and have ridden the appreciation curve, so now they have a lot of equity in their house. Some are getting the trickle-down effect of inheritance. We see a self-selected group, of course: They're conservative enough to have hired a financial planner in the first place. But by and large, most of our clients are going to make it.

Bottom line is, when you go in for your first colonoscopy, review what you want out of life! They're both preventive.

WHAT IS THE DIFFERENCE BETWEEN MEDICARE AND MEDICAID?

People are often confused about the differences between these two programs and who is qualified for which one. Both are medical insurance programs sponsored by the federal government. Both are considered entitlement programs, which means that if you are eligible for the service, you will receive it. You cannot be denied Medicare or Medicaid because of budget shortfalls or lack of available services; there are no waiting lists. However, like any insurance, you are responsible for finding providers who accept it. Before we delve into the politics of the programs, you will need to know the difference between the two.

Medicare is the program primarily associated with Social Security. If you receive Social Security because you are retired (and at least age 65) or because you have a disabling condition, you will automatically receive Medicare. Medicare allows you to choose your own provider and to go to specialists without a referral. One of the drawbacks is that Medicare only pays 80 percent of your medical bills. The cost of health care can really mount up without a secondary insurance, commonly called medigap insurance, that often comes with high premiums but will pay the remaining 20 percent. Out-of-pocket medical costs for healthy people 70 years of age and above is estimated at about two thousand dollars per year without medigap insurance. An estimated 80 percent of people over 65 manage at least one chronic health condition, and their medical costs may soar if there is a health crisis such as cancer or stroke. Because of modern advances in medical care, we are able to live functional lives with conditions that once were an automatic death sentence. But if we (or our parents) can't afford additional health insurance along with our Medicare, many of us may face bankruptcy from stratospheric medical bills.

It pays to read the fine print on Medicare documents to find out what it covers. Like most insurance programs, there are limitations for different situations. For instance, hospital stays for particular conditions are sometimes restricted to a certain number of days. Stay longer, and you are responsible for the balance of the cost. If you require long term care in a skilled-nursing facility, your care must be classified as rehabilitation rather than maintenance, or Medicare will not cover it. Rehab coverage is often limited to three weeks, but some conditions require longer intervention. If you or your parent needs extensive medical intervention and Medicare is the primary payer, ask the hospital staff if they have a medical social worker who can help you manage the economic maze. Their help is reassuring and invaluable.

Medicaid is the health program primarily associated with Supplemental Security Income (SSI) or an extremely low income (or no income at all). SSI is different from Social Security. It is granted to individuals who have a chronic disabling condition, such as a developmental disability or chronic mental illness, and who have no substantial work history from which to draw Social Security. If you are eligible for SSI, you are automatically eligible for Medicaid with full benefits. All medical bills are paid and medications are either free or have very small co-pays. The catch with Medicaid is that, in order to keep full coverage, your income from any source cannot exceed the federally established limit (called the SSI standard), which is an unbelievable $603 per month as of January 2006. Nor can you have any cash savings over $2000. That is a state of poverty, to say the least.

You can have both Medicare and full Medicaid coverage (which will pay the 20 percent not covered by Medicare) if your Social Security is not more than $603 per month. That said, there is also a type of Medicaid that will provide partial coverage if you are poor but exceed the income limit. This program is called a *spend-down* program. The individuals in such a program are required to spend a certain amount of their own money on medical expenses before Medicaid is available. Many applicants can't meet the requirement because they simply do not have enough cash to spend any of it on health care—they need it for food and rent. Since they haven't paid their "share" of the medical bills, they can't get the Medicaid. (Health-care reform, anyone?)

The term *spend down* is also used when a person must exhaust all resources in order to apply for Medicaid. This is a situation that frequently occurs when people, usually seniors, need long term care. If you have parents who are at risk for a long term illness, or if you are yourself, you may want to research the often confounding Medicaid regulations to determine whether you should get long term care insurance for yourself or your mom and dad (see page 172 for more info on long term care insurance). Although Medicaid is a federal program, it is administrated by the individual states, and the rules for eligibility and types of coverage vary. If you or your parents need Medicaid, you will have to apply for it through your local department of social and health services or a qualified social worker.

Both Medicare and Medicaid are frequently in the news, as medical costs skyrocket and public coffers are nearing empty. Again, because they are entitlement programs, the ranks of each swell annually, yet politicians are afraid to take bold steps to solve our health-care woes. What that has meant for the individual consumer is that it is getting harder to find doctors and hospitals that will accept Medicare or Medicaid insurance. Both reimburse doctors at a rate that is established by the government. Doctors complain that these rates are far below their actual costs, and as a result they either refuse to treat Medicare and Medicaid patients or limit the number of such patients.

Medicare patients should know that doctors are allowed to choose whether or not to accept the Medicare rates. They may accept your Medicare insurance, but if the doctor is not a *participating* Medicare provider, that 80 percent of the bill will be a lot higher, because it will be at market rate, not the established Medicare rate. You will pay the difference between the Medicare rate and the doctor's rate out of your own pocket.

No discussion of Medicare and Medicaid would be complete without touching on the new Medicare Part D program. Part D is partial coverage for medications. Although criticized as being confusing and favoring drug companies over consumers, Part D has given many people considerable relief from crushing monthly medication costs. It is, at best, a partial solution to another dizzying problem within our health-care system, but it is worth discussing it with your parents if they have Medicare and any kind of medication costs. Because there are penalties for not signing up, consumers with insignificant drug expenses are urged to get the cheapest plan they can find in order to avoid the penalties. There is a lot of assistance out there for understanding and signing up for Part D. Pharmacies, senior centers, or AARP can help. If you want to delve into the intricacies of Medicare and Medicaid yourself, the Web sites cms.hhs.gov and medicare.gov will give you accurate information from the source.

 THE GOOD NEWS

Beyond Medicare Part D

If you are low-income, underinsured, and not yet eligible for Medicare, there are a number of discount drug programs that can significantly lower your medication costs. Some of them are offered by pharmacies and others by the pharmaceutical companies that manufacture the drugs. You can directly contact the drug companies that produce your medications to find out if you are eligible for their medication assistance program. Or visit the Web site benefitscheckup.org and click on "Benefits CheckupRX."

WHAT IS THE LOOK-BACK LAW?

The look-back law was designed to protect the government from "resource dumping" by citizens who want to safeguard their assets while still qualifying for Medicaid. It came about because of a couple of points I have already mentioned but will repeat for the sake of those who are not reading this chapter at a single sitting, highlighter clutched in hand.

Well-worn point number one: People are living longer, which means the costs of long term care, whether provided in an assisted-living facility or in a nursing home, are going up. Costs can range anywhere from three thousand to seven thousand dollars per month, depending on the type of care and the location of the home. At those prices, a person can demolish a life savings in quick order, and most people are distressed about that. They wouldn't mind providing for their own care in old age if the cost were not so prohibitive, but they resent having to devote every last dollar to end-of-life care. Never mind that they will chuff and wheeze twenty years longer than the generation before them, they would like to leave something to their children, and their children would like that too.

Enter well-worn point number two: If a person is eligible for Medicaid, he or she is entitled to it by law. A few years ago, people figured out that if Mom began putting her assets into someone else's name (usually her children's), she would quickly meet the spend-down requirement of having resources under two thousand dollars and would be eligible for Medicaid to pay for her long term care. Uncle Sam would pay the bill at Creaky Elm Acres, and Mom's life savings would be safely tucked away under Junior's name. And it was all perfectly legal. Well, Uncle Sam is no dummy. The government realized that classifying people with plenty of resources as poverty cases because no assets could be traced to their names would rapidly bankrupt a system set up to serve the indigent. Their answer to resource dumping is the look-back law, or to use its proper name, the look-back period.

The look-back period is part of the Federal Budget Reconciliation Law. It is rather simple. When a person applies for Medicaid for the purposes of long term facility care, the government will look back for five years prior to the application to find out if the person has transferred assets. If there have been any asset transfers within that period, the government will apply a mathematical formula to the amount transferred, and your start date for receiving Medicaid will be delayed based on the results. The more assets you have transferred, the longer your start date will be delayed. It is easy to rack up large bills over only a few weeks, so the delay could be quite costly.

Medicaid is also allowed to collect money from the estate of a deceased person if any assets were in his name during the look back period. Typically, this would be money from the sale of a home. A home is not considered an asset if you live in it. Many people who need nursing-home care are cash-poor and are eligible for Medicaid even if they own their own house. *Once they move into a nursing home, the house is considered an asset and Medicaid may put a lien on it to collect for medical bills after it is sold.*

People who want to be a jump ahead of the look-back period must plan very carefully. Many assisted-living facilities and nursing homes are getting picky about accepting residents who come in on Medicaid. Like the family doctor, long term care facilities must accept the rates set by the government for cost of care and—you guessed it—facilities are complaining that the Medicaid reimbursement rates are lower than their actual costs. They prefer private-pay clients and, increasingly, they are asking for financial proof that a potential resident can pay for one to three years of care before he spends down and must go on Medicaid. More commonly, facilities are designating fewer and fewer beds to Medicaid clients, and the waiting lists to get into a given facility can be months.

The average stay in both assisted-living facilities and nursing homes is just under two years. It is obvious from these emerging financial restrictions that the management is hoping to avoid Medicaid patients. In other words, if your parents are planning on transferring assets way ahead of time they will find that, in the end, money talks, and they need to be careful that whoever they transfer the money *to* still regards the money as theirs. Your mom and dad may need that cash to get the care they actually want, rather than getting stuck with very few options because of Medicaid.

WHAT'S THE DIFFERENCE BETWEEN ESSENTIAL AND NONESSENTIAL DEBT?

There have been a lot of warnings in the news lately about how the boomer generation has the worst savings record in history. As the trend moves away from employer-sponsored retirement plans, and individuals are increasingly pressured to manage their own retirement, the picture worsens. Most people are not savvy investors, and many don't make enough money to put much away after their monthly expenses. Add to that an extended life span after retirement, along with the increasing costs of housing, food, utilities, and medical care, and soon many people will have the same epitaph: "He died at his desk." For those who are limping along, doing OK, it only takes one medical crisis to trigger a financial squeeze that feels like a vise.

The first step in wiggling out of the bind is to take a hard look at essential debt and nonessential debt and make a plan. Essential debt is defined as the essential bills one must pay in order to live. Rent or mortgage, utilities, food, and taxes make up the core of essential debt. Not paying these bills will result in dire consequences, so they must be paid first, regardless of other pressures. Items such as car and health insurance are not essential to living, but it is a gamble to neglect those bills because the policies may lapse. Secured loans (with property as collateral) are not considered essential either, but nonpayment can result in seizure of the property.

Reducing essential debt is often possible by making some changes that are uncomfortable but may be more practical in the long run: moving to a cheaper home, applying for public assistance, making some dietary changes that lean heavily toward the vegetarian, or asking the IRS for a payment plan for outstanding taxes. Many people are resistant to these changes for all the obvious emotional and psychological reasons. But *essential* is the operative word here. It may be essential to make these adjustments in order to make it through a rough period and survive to enjoy steak another day.

Unessential debts are the bills that, if gone unpaid, will not result in dire consequences. These include credit cards, subscriptions, cable, personal loans, and department-store bills. People live in dread of being turned over to collection agencies for unpaid credit-card bills, and those agencies take harassment to dizzying heights, but in reality they can do very little to harm you. The harm amounts to these unpaid bills appearing on your credit record for seven years. If you live on Social Security and/or a pension, that money is untouchable by law. Sometimes writing a letter to a collection agency and letting them know that your income is only Social Security will get them off your back. Often it won't. You can negotiate with a collection agency for a lowered minimum payment, but think carefully about that. If the new minimum payment only goes toward penalty fees and interest and is never applied toward the principal, it is not worth taking money away from essential debt to make the payment, because you are never actually lowering your debt! Not paying the bill makes better financial sense.

Don't let shame keep you from being a savvy negotiator. Negotiating with collection agencies is seldom fruitful, but if you contact the companies that you actually owe money to, they may be willing to bargain. For example, say you owe a computer retailer a thousand dollars. Before they turn you over to collections, call them. Let them know you are in financial straits and what your income is. They're not stupid—they may recognize that once this bill gets to collections they won't get a dime, so if you offer them five hundred dollars to settle the debt, they just may go for it.

If you're not the type to haggle with creditors or you feel too overwhelmed by your situation, you might hire a credit counselor to help you create a plan and do the negotiating for you. Shop for a counselor carefully; some are con artists who will take your cash, ostensibly to pay your bills, and disappear with it. The Association of Independent Consumer Credit Counseling Agencies (aiccca.org) and the National Foundation for Credit Counseling (nfcc.org) have directories of counselors who are supposed to adhere to certain standards, but being listed is not a guarantee of the counselor's honesty. Before hiring one, check with the Better Business Bureau or the state attorney general's office to make sure no complaints have been filed against the person.

SHOULD I FILE FOR BANKRUPTCY?

What if it's all too much? What if you don't want to spend your last good years hunched over a calculator, mumbling obscenities? The word *bankruptcy*, once tainted with humiliation and failure, might start sounding pretty good. Some of the tarnish of bankruptcy has worn off over the last few years, what with respected corporations like the major airlines, Sprint, IBM, and Winn-Dixie reorganizing under Chapter 11.

Maybe you're broke because you were laid off during one of these reorganizations. Why shouldn't the little guy take advantage of bankruptcy as well?

As a matter of fact, over the past twenty years, bankruptcy has become a growing trend (or necessity). There were 300,000 personal bankruptcies filed in 1980, and the number climbed to a staggering 2,100,000 by 2005. A change in the bankruptcy laws in October 2005 put the brakes on this steady climb, and after a surge of filers right before the law changed, the number has dropped dramatically. Needless to say, the change in the laws makes it more difficult to file.

The allure of bankruptcy is having one's debts erased and getting a fresh start. But it is not quite that simple. What bankruptcy can generally do for you is to wipe out credit-card debt and the harassment associated with it, plus erase any other unsecured debt. Unsecured debt is debt that has not been secured with collateral, so the creditor cannot put a lien on or repossess your property. A bankruptcy will also stop any legal proceedings begun by these types of creditors. Most people seeking bankruptcy do so because their credit-card debt has skyrocketed out of control, but that does not necessarily mean they are shopaholics with poor impulse control. Two out of three filers have lost a job, and 50 percent have faced a major medical crisis. Credit cards have often been the only way to manage.

What bankruptcy cannot do is wipe out secured debt, child support or alimony payments, debts associated with criminal retribution such as DUI fines, or any debt that was incurred due to financial fraud. If you have large payments associated with these expenses, a bankruptcy might not make much difference to your situation. Because bankruptcy forces an individual to bare all his personal financial information to public scrutiny, and it will remain on his record for ten years (making credit difficult to obtain), it should not be taken lightly.

The new bankruptcy laws have made the process a bit more painful. Generally, individuals choose either a Chapter 7 bankruptcy or a Chapter 13 filing, based on their financial circumstances. Chapter 7 often eliminates more debt, because Chapter 13 is reserved for individuals with some steady income and has the expectation that the debtor will pay some debt out of that income. However, Chapter 7 will not stop a foreclosure as Chapter 13 will, and there is an expectation in Chapter 7 that all nonexempt property will be sold and go toward the elimination of some of the debt. You are allowed to keep your nonexempt property under Chapter 13. Exempt property is the property that the law allows you *not* to count as part of your financial assets. What qualifies as exempt varies from state to state.

For people with higher incomes who would have chosen Chapter 7, the new law has tighter restrictions. First, you must average all your income over the last six months and compare it to the median income for a family of your size for your state. (Remember, *median* is not the average income but what falls right in the middle of the range). If your average income is equal to or less than the median, you can file for Chapter 7—*if* you pass a means test. The means test is a formula that subtracts allowed expenses (not necessarily *your* expenses but expenses set by the IRS) plus the payments you make for secured or necessary debts (such as child support or wages to employees) from your income. If, after all this subtracting, your monthly disposable income is $100 or less, you have passed the means test and can file under Chapter 7. If your disposable income is between $100 and $166.66, you have more math in your future. You must further ascertain if this amount of monthly disposable income can pay more than 25 percent of your unessential debt over a five-year period. If it can, then Chapter 7 is not an option. Information on the means test and state median incomes can be found at usdoj.gov/ust.

Both Chapter 7 and Chapter 13 now require credit counseling before anyone can file for bankruptcy. (The above Web site also contains information about credit counseling agencies that are approved by Uncle Sam.) The credit counselor will examine your financial situation in great detail, will make a recommendation whether filing for bankruptcy is actually beneficial to you, and will make a plan for repayment of your debts. You are not obligated to follow this plan, but for individuals who will go on to file under Chapter 13, the plan is quite helpful. As mentioned earlier, Chapter 13 filers are expected to pay some of their debt. The court will monitor the repayment plan, and a court-appointed trustee will administer all the individual's income for three to five years. In addition, the trustee is entitled to a commission out of the individual's income, resulting in further reduction of the money earmarked toward the debt.

Whew. There is a lot to consider before making this leap. Another significant consideration for the financially squeezed is whether to retain a lawyer for bankruptcy proceedings. Because of the intricacies of the law, it is highly recommended to have a lawyer manage this process. However, the new bankruptcy laws now require lawyers to personally guarantee that all of the information provided to them by clients is accurate, so fees have gone up. Some bankruptcy lawyers are abandoning this type of law altogether, making good ones harder to find. Legal aide societies can provide some assistance to help you through the process, but it won't be like retaining a personal lawyer. If your situation is very simple—you own no significant property, have very little income, and mainly have credit-card debt—legal aide may be all you need. It makes sense to go through the required credit counseling before making the decision to hire a lawyer or to use legal aide.

So, should you file for bankruptcy? Take a good look at your situation. The average filer is 38 years old. Chances are, he has a young family and a lot of working years left ahead of him. It may be very necessary to get out from under the debt in order to move forward. If you are close to retirement age or are past retirement, if you don't require good credit to start another business venture, and if you basically just want to live within your means, bankruptcy may not be that advantageous. Sure, it will relieve the nagging pressure of debt that can erode one's quality of life, but if you can't afford bankruptcy, think carefully before you proceed. As mentioned earlier, the consequences of unpaid nonessential debt are bad credit, the same as bankruptcy. Bankruptcy relieves you of the nagging feeling, but for the most part you still don't pay the debt, so what has been gained? If you own a home with significant equity, you can often use a reverse mortgage to pay your debts. The point is, don't make the decision based on panic or fear but on the facts and, if possible, the input of a financially savvy adviser.

six

THE FUTURE

WHAT ARE THE TOP VACATION CHOICES FOR PEOPLE OVER 40?

It's an interesting paradox: In a 2005 survey, travelers age 41 to 59 claimed that their top priority for a vacation is that it is set in a "beautiful scenic place." Yet the same survey found that the destination these people actually visit more than any other is Las Vegas. Scenic beauty indeed—if the Styxlike indoor waterways of the Venetian Hotel, with its ominous twenty-four-hour twilight, counts as beautiful.

At any rate, travel marketers are drooling at the prospect of an aging, childless, freewheeling boomer boom in travel over the next twenty-five years, and they're falling all over themselves trying to figure out how we'll want to spend our cash. According to the industry, the following trends have emerged.

We like to travel with family and friends, but we're not too keen on meeting new people. Cruises and family reunions are in, group tours are out, unless the tour offers an exotic trip we can't arrange on our own. Many midlifers enjoy traveling with their children and grandchildren, which has resulted in a surge of popularity for resorts like Club Med, where meals are included and the children have their own activities. Among those currently favored are Punta Cana, in the Dominican Republic, and the many all-inclusives in the Caribbean and on Mexico's Mayan Riviera. Tauck World Discovery's Web site describes its all-inclusive family packages as "carefully crafted journeys [that] combine the joy of seeing, doing and learning as a family with ample opportunity for just plain family fun." *Seeing, doing,* and *learning* are the buzzwords midlifers want to hear, according to marketers, because we're not passive. Unless we're at a spa.

We like to vacation with people our own age, not with a bunch of geezers (anyone older than us). The Association of Travel Marketing Executives advises, "The industry can respond to these needs by not mixing age groups in the same tour and using younger words and images in their marketing material." How much gray should pepper the full head of hair on that strapping fiftyish hiker? How many delicate lines should crease the beautiful, vibrant face of that sixty-something woman? It's fun to watch the marketers struggle to find an image that will inspire us without making us feel too old and fat to join the club.

We like having things arranged for us. We don't want to hassle with details. This may be because most of us are still working, and many will have to keep on working long after we turn 60. Our vacation days are precious, so no matter how exotic the locale, we don't want to waste our time lugging bags, waiting in lines, or trying to figure out the activity options after we arrive. If the whole vacation can be put on a single credit card charge, so much the better. The all-inclusive resorts and cruises have been wise to this for a long time; now other travel retailers are offering all-inclusive versions of riverboat cruises, rail journeys, and just about everything in between. The price typically includes meals, alcoholic and nonalcoholic beverages, entertainment, tips and gratuities, airport transfers, and some activities.

We like new experiences. Preoccupation with our health prevents us from pursuing the highs of yesteryear, so instead we seek vacations that offer adventure, physical challenges, or spiritual renewal. Adventure needn't mean kayaking or rock climbing, which many of us claim to crave but are secretly too chicken to try. It can mean watching wildlife (whales, bison, moose, bears, birds), cycling through the Loire Valley (nice and flat), and snorkeling with dolphins (Australia's Monkey Mia Dolphin Resort promises dolphins that are "wild, native to the area and visit of their own accord. With an attendance record of 99.6%, they are the most reliable dolphins in the world!"). Fitness vacations cater to those of us who feel guilty if we stop exercising for even a few days: We can sign up for boot camps, weight-training sessions, and yoga regimens, interrupted by plentiful helpings of spa cuisine. For spiritual tune-ups, we can walk Spain's Camino de Santiago, take a "soul adventure" in Sedona, Arizona, or retreat to the silence of a Zen monastery anywhere from Japan to New York. The options are truly breathtaking. It's also worth mentioning that some monasteries offer low nightly rates in exchange for working a few hours. At Tassajara Zen Mountain Center in Northern California, current rates are fifty-five dollars plus three hours of work a day (nonwork rates are also available).

We like new places. It's becoming rare for people to return to a destination even once, much less year after year like our parents did. Because many of us traveled in our youth, we've already seen the major tourist spots. Specialty travel agencies are luring our jaded selves with deals that will take us diving in the Maldives, scootering through Tuscany, or cruising Lake Titicaca on a reed boat. But wherever we go . . .

We like to be pampered. We want gourmet cuisine, fresh sheets, hot showers, and someone to clean up after us. With few exceptions, this generation is not into roughing it. Writing in *Specialty Travel* magazine about her tour through the Grand Tetons on a covered wagon, Bridget Cook noted that the wagons were "fitted with rubberized wheels and padded seats for comfort." Cowboys set up tents for sleeping. "At dinnertime each night, everyone gathered eagerly for the chuck-wagon feasts: Dutch-oven ham, bacon, potatoes, roasts, chicken, fresh homemade rolls, stews, salads, sumptuous desserts and a variety of beverages." After dinner, the travelers were treated to guitar and fiddle tunes, roping lessons, and an "old timer" who spun Western yarns for their entertainment. It ain't backpacking with a Coleman stove, but it sure sounds like fun.

ODD ARCHIVES ——————————————

The region is, of course, altogether valueless. It can be approached only from the south, and after entering it there is nothing to do but leave. Ours has been the first, and will doubtless be the last party of whites to visit this profitless locality.

—Lieutenant Joseph C. Ives describing the Grand Canyon, from his "Report upon the Colorado River of the West," 1858.

ARE RVS COOL YET?

No one would deny the inherent coolness of vintage Airstream trailers, those silver bullets with shipshape wooden interiors. Airstreams are still being manufactured, only now they come with stainless steel appliances, adorable retro screen doors, and Jetson-style fold-up computers (be mine, Safari Bambi edition). If you can't decide whether RVs are the natural domain of wobbly oldsters or the natural evolution of the party van, check out an RV show in your area. You will be stunned by the variety of recreational vehicles designed for every taste and nearly every budget. (Rvtrader.com lists annual events nationwide.)

The RV industry is enjoying record growth, due both to the swelling boomer market and to the RV's appeal to young families. According to a 2005 study by the University of Michigan's Survey Research Center, one in twelve U.S. vehicle-owning households owns at least one RV. It's not the elderly who are buying most feverishly: 35- to 54-year-olds make up the largest segment of the market. The appeal for midlifers lies in the flexibility and relative afford-ability of vacationing in an RV, although rising gasoline prices may put a damper on that in the future. The vehicles range from land yachts boasting Italian marble bathrooms and Corinthian leather sofas, to the nifty Airstreams, to Class C motor homes, the industry workhorses.

Like other travel retailers, proprietors of RV camp-grounds are catching on to our generation's love of the finer things. No longer are we forced to use a rickety wooden restroom and wash our pots in a cold water sink located just outside the loo. Some campgrounds now feature swimming pools, evening entertainment programs, tennis courts, golf courses, health spas, and Internet access. There are campgrounds near popular tourist attractions and remote campgrounds offering rustic amenities along with spectacular scenery. That's perhaps the biggest ad-vantage of the RV—you can design just about any vacation you like.

There are drawbacks, however. Taking an RV trip re-quires a lot of preparation, from sanitizing the tanks to sup-plying the vehicle with fresh water, food, cooking utensils, bedding, bath and laundry supplies, and so on. If you can't keep the RV in your driveway, you'll be paying for storage as well. Maintenance is also a factor, and in this area many RV owners have been unhappily surprised when they purchase a new vehicle, according to Tom Gonser, who with his wife Stephanie founded the Web site rversonline.org. New RVs often require a lot of "corrective" work, writes Gonser, which has resulted in "a tendency among many knowledgeable RVers (former owners) to 'buy used'—and avoid the frustration and downtime that purchase of a new RV can entail." Service on the vehicles is notoriously unpredictable and time-consuming: "It appears that qualified RV technicians are in short supply."

For a price, you can avoid all the hassle and enjoy high-end RV travel. The latest trend in RVing is "fractional ownership," a strategy first employed by folks who wanted to own a private jet but couldn't quite make the monthly payments. American Quarter Coach, manufacturers of luxury RVs, has launched a similar plan in which RVs worth $250,000 to over $1 million are sold in shares of one-eighth (five weeks annual usage) to one half (twenty-four weeks). The agreement usually lasts for three years, upon which the used RV is sold and the participants split the proceeds. Aside from getting to travel in a "palace on wheels," owners receive the RV fully stocked and prepped for each trip. The company will deliver it to your doorstep or to any city in the United States, so you can fly across country, pick up your road-ready RV, and take off.

The less privileged can simply rent an RV to find out how the road feels after all these years. Rversonline.org, one of the few RV Web sites not sponsored by the industry, offers nearly two thousand well-organized pages of information provided by RVers themselves. It's an invaluable first stop on any RV journey.

HOW CAN I ASK MY PARENTS ABOUT THEIR MONEY?

Most adults don't like to talk with their parents about sex, death, or money. However, if you're old enough to be reading this book, you probably need to discuss finances with your mom and dad. You may end up touching on mortality as well, but if you're lucky, no one will mention sex.

There are plenty of reasons to have the financial chat sooner rather than later. People are living longer these days, which means you may end up assisting your parents financially, physically, or both. Therefore, even though their assets may seem like none of your business, that's not quite the case unless they are so wealthy that you will never be called upon to lend them a hand. A 2005 survey by Pew Research Center found that about 30 percent of midlifers are helping their parents financially (another 19 percent receive money *from* their folks).

Many people only learn about their parents' financial situation when their mother or father dies or becomes seriously ill. Then they find out that Dad handled all the money, and Mom doesn't know where the accounts are; or the retirement fund was insufficient, so Mom and Dad have been racking up credit-card debt; or it's been two years since Mom deposited any rent checks from that apartment building she owns. The time to help your parents sort things out is now, while they can still remember where they keep the files (or paper bags stuffed with receipts) and explain their system to you. If you wait until a crisis to have this discussion, not only will you have one more burden during a time of great stress, but you may be too distraught to make rational decisions.

Another reason to talk to your parents about their money is that, if they neglect to do things like write a will, set up a living trust, or appoint someone power of attorney, it can end up costing them and you thousands of dollars in legal fees and taxes that could have been avoided. Failing to draw up these essential documents can have other unintended consequences, such as assets from a first marriage going to the stepchildren of a second marriage.

Typically, seniors who are reluctant to talk with their adult children about estate planning are scared. They are afraid of losing control over their money (which they believe means losing control over their life), afraid of thinking about illness and death, afraid of revealing their savings or lack thereof, afraid of children whom they don't quite trust, afraid of setting off fights among their children. In order for the conversation to be fruitful, you will need to preserve your parents' dignity and calm their fears. In many families, there is one sibling who gets along especially well with the parents and who should probably be tapped as spokesperson for the clan, as long as everyone trusts him or her.

Sometimes a life event, such as retirement, recovering from an illness, or selling a home, provides a good opening for the financial chat. If you don't have that excuse, you can use the information-exchange approach: "Mom and Dad, I've collected all my important papers, and I want to discuss them with you so you can help manage things if anything should happen to me. I'd like to know where your records are, too." If your parents don't have their estate in order, it's a good time to suggest that they go to a financial planner. (If there is any mistrust between you, they or a third party should select the planner. Otherwise you could end up getting blamed for less-than-stellar financial advice.) If you are on good terms with your folks, you could ask to accompany them to the meeting. And if you don't have your own estate in order, you might want to hire someone who specializes in intergenerational financial planning. That person can then be the one to bring up potentially touchy subjects such as long term care insurance and living wills.

In addition to reviewing your parents' income and charting a course for their financial future, a good planner will raise the following topics, which are discussed in detail in chapter 5:

- Will and living trust.
- Living will. This tells the hospital and doctors what type of life support, if any, your parent wants in case of a life threatening illness or accident.
- Medical and financial power of attorney. This gives another person the legal power to make medical and financial decisions for your parent.

As part of your exchange, you and your parents should share the information listed below. You don't have to divulge the cash value of your bank accounts and investments; you just have to tell them where the files are, so they can find them if you get flattened by an SUV or otherwise felled by untimely misfortune.

- Social Security number
- Medicare number
- Insurance policies: home, health, car, life, and long term care
- Health records
- Names and phone numbers of financial advisor, accountant, attorney, and doctors
- Will and/or living trust
- Living will
- Monthly bills and debts
- Tax returns
- Safe deposit box location and keys
- Bank accounts and investment portfolios

According to the Financial Planning Association, certain behaviors should alert you that a parent needs financial intervention right away. Talk to your parents now if they have expressed worry about paying their bills; if you discover that they are sending contributions to dubious charities or contests; if they have been notified by the IRS that they haven't paid their taxes correctly; if you find unpaid bills or undeposited checks around their house; or if you learn that they are investing in financial products that strike you as too risky.

WHAT ARE THE CHANCES THAT I'LL BE A CAREGIVER?

It is estimated that at least 22 million Americans are currently caring for a loved one who is 50 or older. About 61 percent of these caregivers are women; 39 percent, men. Among women ages 18 to 65 who are taking care of family members, only 18 percent are caring for children, while 83 percent are caring for another adult. More than half of those women are caring for a parent or parent-in-law. Nearly three out of four live with the person for whom they are caring.

The stats differ from study to study, but together they provide overwhelming evidence that many women and quite a few men will spend a good part of their lives caring for at least one elderly relative. Although the longevity gap between males and females is closing, women still outlive men by an average of 5.4 years, which means that wives will most likely care for their aging or ailing husbands as well as their mothers and/or fathers. Men help with caregiving more than they used to, but women remain on the front lines.

These odds can be hard to accept, which may be why a MetLife survey found that most people caring for a 50-plus family member expected to do so for two years or less. Two years seems achievable. You might even be able to pull it off graciously. But contrary to their expectations, the survey respondents ended up caregiving for an average of eight years, not two. A third of the respondents cared for their senior relatives ten years or more. Another survey found that the average duration of caregiving was between one and four years, with about 20 percent lasting five years or longer. While the emotional rewards are significant, and most baby boomers believe that caring for their parents personally is the right thing to do, it would be a mistake to underestimate the toll caregiving may take on your psychological well-being, physical health, and ability to perform your job.

Two words of advice: financial planning (see the previous question). A few more words: Long term care insurance for your parents and perhaps you and your spouse. It's not cheap, but the healthier (and younger) you are when you get it, the more reasonable the rates are. Long term care insurance kicks in when the insured meets certain qualifications, usually regarding one's inability to conduct at least two essential daily tasks, such as dressing or bathing. The insurance not only covers the cost of assisted-living facilities and nursing homes, it also pays for health workers to provide in-home care, which means that you'll have a lot more options if you or someone you love needs help. (See chapter 5 for more information about long term care insurance.)

HOW MUCH WILL IT COST TO SEND MY CHILD TO COLLEGE?

The cost of college tuition pushes the panic button for most midlife parents. It causes us to look at our teenagers not as human beings but as "coulda beens"—coulda been a contender for a slew of scholarships, if only he or she had excelled at one more extracurricular, shot a few more baskets, written a better essay, scored a few points higher on the SAT . . . but this way lies madness. Although the cost of college tuition continues to rise, there is also a rising tide of grants, tuition and fee adjustments, tax breaks, scholarships, and student loans that, taken together, make the process less painful than you might fear.

First, the facts thus far: As of 2006, college tuition and fees at private four-year colleges had risen an average of 5.7 percent *every year* over the previous decade. Tuition and fees at public four-year colleges rose 6.9 percent, and at public two-year colleges they rose 5.1 percent. There is no reason to believe the trend will change. Adjusting for inflation, the cost of going to college is about three times what it was in the 1970s.

The reasons for this are complex and probably don't matter much to you, the strapped parent. But it's worth mentioning that, while colleges would like the public to believe they must raise tuition because of declining state appropriations, overall those appropriations actually rose by 44 percent between 1990 and 2004. Many experts agree that a more accurate picture has to include the funds colleges spend on hiring additional faculty (the rate of new hires has risen more than the rate of student enrollment); additional administrative staff (it has grown even more than the faculty); athletic subsidies; and the glut of new labs, facilities, classrooms, student unions, and fancy dormitories (which the schools say the students demand). According to Richard Vedder, author of *Going Broke by Degree: Why College Costs*

Too Much (AEI Press, 2004), "Remarkably little of the higher spending has gone toward instruction: perhaps 21 cents for each new dollar per student since 1976."

Another troubling development is that some schools have cut back on need-based scholarships and are awarding more merit-based scholarships. According to a 2007 *Los Angeles Times* article by Peter Hong, "By using discounts [merit-based scholarships] to attract students with high grades and test scores, these colleges . . . have enhanced their status in all-important rankings such as the *U.S. News & World Report* list." In other words, colleges are essentially bribing bright students to enroll so that the school's ranking will go up, regardless of whether or not those students are financially needy. A 2004 report by the Century Foundation found that at the 146 most selective colleges in the United States, a mere 3 percent of students come from the nation's lowest socioeconomic quarter, while 74 percent come from its wealthiest.

Raging against the system won't help your college-bound child, unfortunately. But there are other things that will. The main point to remember is that most students (and their families) don't pay full tuition at either private or public colleges. According to The College Board, they pay only about 60 percent of the full cost, after factoring in grants from federal and state governments, institutions, and private sources. Private-school students get an average of about $9,600 a year from these sources, reducing their tuition and fees from an average of $21,235 to $11,600. Public-school students reap about $3,300 in the same benefits, reducing their annual tuition and fees from an average of $5,491 to $2,200. How much you get depends on many factors, from your child's academic standing to your family's income, but the bottom line is that those who diligently look for the money are likely to find it. You will have to run a gauntlet of research and paperwork that could rival any college course, but it's worth the effort. There are dozens of books, Web sites, and counselors (high-school and private) who can help you find the funds.

Schools in the Southwest tend to cost the least, while those on the East Coast are the priciest. The table on page 216, reprinted from *Trends in College Pricing 2006* (The College Board, New York), lists average 2006–2007 student expenses for tuition and fees, room and board, books and supplies, transportation, and other costs. These are the prices before factoring in student aid, grants, and so forth.

Where do most families get the cash to fund this endeavor? Here are the basics of college funding.

Federal grants are awarded based on financial need. There are two types: Pell Grants, which for the 2004–2005 school year ranged from $400 to $4,050, and Federal Supplemental Educational Opportunity Grants (FSEOGs), which ranged from $100 to $4,000. Two new federal grants were added for the 2006–2007 school year: the Academic Competitiveness Grant and the National SMART Grant. SMART stands for Science and Mathematics Access to Retain Talent. It's for third- and fourth-year math and science majors.

Your child's eligibility for federal grants is determined by filling out a Free Application for Federal Student Aid

AVERAGE STUDENT EXPENSES, BY COLLEGE BOARD REGION, 2006–07 (ENROLLMENT-WEIGHTED)

	TUITION & FEES	ADDITIONAL OUT-OF-STATE CHARGES*	BOOKS & SUPPLIES	Resident			Commuter		
				ROOM & BOARD	TRANS-PORTATION	OTHER COSTS	ROOM & BOARD**	TRANS-PORTATION	OTHER COSTS
National									
2-yr public	$2,272	$4,208	$850	——	——	——	$6,299	$1,197	$1,676
4-yr public	$5,836	$9,947	$942	$6,960	$880	$1,739	$6,917	$1,224	$2,048
4-yr private	$22,218		$935	$8,149	$722	$1,277	$7,211	$1,091	$1,630
New England									
2-yr public	$3,363	$6,143	$779	——	——	——	$6,251	$1,108	$1,600
4-yr public	$7,658	$11,128	$848	$7,611	$522	$1,257	$6,495	$923	$1,493
4-yr private	$28,386		$896	$9,726	$573	$1,141	$8,132	$871	$1,223
Middle States									
2-yr public	$3,483	$3,492	$828	——	——	——	$6,607	$1,099	$1,516
4-yr public	$6,860	$8,314	$938	$7,817	$660	$1,607	$6,946	$989	$2,112
4-yr private	$23,327		$905	$9,217	$581	$1,179	$8,064	$1,024	$1,466
South									
2-yr public	$2,176	$4,835	$817	——	——	——	$5,776	$1,364	$1,474
4-yr public	$4,739	$11,003	$877	$6,113	$1,097	$1,673	$6,356	$1,382	$1,883
4-yr private	$19,455		$917	$7,112	$963	$1,423	$6,600	$1,290	$1,868
Midwest									
2-yr public	$2,831	$3,549	$817	——	——	——	$5,335	$1,272	$1,608
4-yr public	$7,075	$10,048	$828	$6,399	$793	$1,850	$6,201	$1,122	$2,089
4-yr private	$20,793		$938	$6,967	$709	$1,204	$6,229	$1,131	$1,831
Southwest									
2-yr public	$1,702	$3,028	$755	——	——	——	——	$1,380	$1,571
4-yr public	$5,462	$7,300	$918	$6,045	$1,226	$1,932	$5,992	$1,594	$2,059
4-yr private	$18,280		$935	$6,558	$925	$1,396	$5,812	$1,210	$1,498
West									
2-yr public	$1,309	$4,603	$967	——	——	——	$7,269	$1,010	$2,024
4-yr public	$4,646	$10,526	$1,187	$8,753	$930	$1,905	$8,417	$1,212	$2,199
4-yr private	$21,765		$1,073	$8,409	$707	$1,656	$7,568	$975	$1,651

*The average out-of-state tuition and fee charges are computed as the sum of the enrollment-weighted average in-state tuition and fees plus the average out-of-state premium, weighted by full-time out-of-state enrollments in each institution.
**Room and board costs for commuter students are average estimated living expenses for students living off campus but not with parents as reported by institutions in the Annual Survey of Colleges.
Dashes indicate that the sample was too small to provide meaningful information.
Source. "Trends in College Pricing 2006" Copyright © 2006 The College Board, www.collegeboard.com. Reproduced with permission.

(FAFSA). Go to fafsa.ed.gov for complete instructions. All students, no matter what their family income, should fill out a FAFSA. Depending on the tuition at your child's school, he or she may qualify for aid even if your annual income is above $100,000. The federal government's student-aid Web site, student aid.ed.gov, is a good place to start on your journey to funding.

State grants. Each state has its own menu of grants. To locate the Web site for your state's grant program, go to studentaid.ed.gov, click on "Funding," scroll down that page until you see the link "state higher education agency," and click on that. It will take you to a list of all the states and their funding sites.

College scholarships. Each college and university offers its students scholarships. (Note: fewer than 1 percent of students receive athletic scholarships. Forty-nine percent receive need- or merit-based scholarships.) At many schools, the amount of the scholarship is tied to the student's SAT score—a higher score gets more cash. Numerous Web sites are devoted to helping students figure out the scholarships offered by various schools. Fastweb.com and findtuition.com are two of the most popular. Individual schools' Web sites will also give you the information on their financial aid page.

Corporate scholarships. Coca-Cola makes you smarter. No? Well, Coca-Cola does pay you for being smarter. The company hands out 250 scholarships a year, 50 for twenty thousand dollars and 200 for four thousand dollars. It is just one of many businesses that sponsor college scholarships. Find the others on search sites such as scholarships.com.

Federal work-study programs. The government awards many schools a fund for work-study programs. Through the program, qualifying students may work part-time, usually on campus. Work-study funds are not a bottomless well of money, however. When a school's allotment is used up, no more work-study jobs will be awarded that year.

Workforce-contingent financial aid (WCFA) programs. These are state-funded programs that help pay for college expenses in exchange for work, either in specific fields or at specific locations. Most of the programs stipulate that you must be a resident of the state where the school is located. In-school WCFA programs are the most common, accounting for 90 percent of all awards. These support the student while he or she is in school, usually in exchange for a commitment that, upon graduation, the student will work in a particular field in that state for a certain number of years. On-the-job WCFAs repay student loans in exchange for a similar commitment. Students studying to be teachers account for 69 percent of WCFA recipients; other fields include nursing, engineering, technology, medicine, dentistry, and optometry.

529 savings plans. These are state-sponsored college savings accounts. Your child does *not* have to attend a college in the state that sponsors the plan, and you don't have to use a plan offered by the state you live in—you can choose any state's plan. The money you contribute to the 529 plan is managed either by the state treasurer's office or by an outside investment firm. The interest on your investment grows tax-free, and it will not be federally taxed as long as your child uses it for college expenses.

Coverdell education savings accounts. Parents can contribute up to two thousand dollars a year to these accounts and earnings will accumulate tax-free. The money won't be taxed if it is withdrawn for tuition or other college-related expenses.

IRAs. If you are really strapped for college cash, you can raid your own IRA. You won't be charged the usual 10 percent penalty if the money is used for your child's college expenses.

The Hope Scholarship Tax Credit. Some families qualify for a Hope credit, a federal income tax credit worth up to $1,500 per student per year. The maximum a family can earn and still qualify changes each year. IRS publication 970 explains the rules. Find it at irs.gov/publications/p970.

Federal Student Loans. The federal government sponsors a number of loans for students and their parents. The Web site studentaid.ed.gov outlines the options. You are allowed between ten and thirty years to repay, depending on the type of loan.

College-bound teenagers should be warned *not* to fund their education with credit cards. Credit-card companies prey on students, setting up tables on campuses and offering free T-shirts, coffee mugs, and water bottles to anyone who fills out an application. Many colleges are happy to let students pay their tuition with a credit card—they don't care about the exorbitant interest rates. Before your child goes off to college, try to educate him or her about the dangers of plastic.

THE GOOD NEWS —————————————————

Ivy League Not Required

For decades the Ivy League—Brown, Columbia, Cornell, Dartmouth, Harvard, University of Pennsylvania, Princeton, and Yale—has been the Holy Grail for parents. It remains that way for many who believe that a degree from an Ivy League school will assure their children success and job security in an unstable world. But an Ivy League degree offers no such guarantee.

Since the 1980s, various studies have been conducted to determine what happens to Ivy League graduates in terms of job success and salary. Even back in 1980, Ivy grads accounted for only 14 percent of CEOs at Fortune 100 companies. By 2001, it was down to 10 percent. In 2004, there were 99 new CEOs at Fortune 1000 companies, and only eight of them were graduates of Ivy League schools. Even more telling, five of those eight attended Harvard's Advanced Management Program, an intensive ten-week course that costs a staggering $52,500 and allows the graduate to put "Harvard" on his or her résumé.

What about eventual earnings? In 1999, researchers Alan Krueger and Stacy Berg Dale announced that an Ivy League degree was not the deciding factor in potential income. The researchers had surveyed a group of students who in 1976 had been admitted to elite schools but chose to go elsewhere, and compared them to a group the same age that had attended the Ivies. Nearly twenty years later, members of both groups were making essentially the same salaries. The common denominator was that these students were intelligent and driven enough to be accepted at the top schools, not that they actually attended them. Most studies, education specialists, employers, and employment recruiters have reached the same conclusion: Success depends on determination, talent, and intelligence, not on where you got your degree.

Some corporate recruiters have shifted their efforts to non-Ivy campuses because of unsettling attributes common to Ivy League grads, including a sense of entitlement that is not always supported by their on-the-job performance. Ivy grads tend to switch jobs often and to overestimate their worth. What's more, an Ivy League degree can be off-putting to the people who are hiring if they did not attend an elite school. And many employers feel that the hothouse atmosphere of the Ivy League isn't the best place to cull leaders who must deal with a workforce that is ethnically and economically diverse.

There is no denying that students get a good education at Ivy League colleges and that the prestigious name and the connections a student makes at such a school can open doors when he or she first joins the workforce. In the long run, however, it is performance that counts.

In recent years, *U.S. News and World Report*'s list of the top 100 colleges has joined the Ivy League as a font of anxiety for parents and high-school seniors. At least it is comprised of a hundred schools, not just eight. If you would like another perspective, Loren Pope, author of

Colleges That Change Lives (Penguin, 2006), has compiled a list of non-elite schools he believes provide a top-notch education. Find it at ctcl.com.

WHAT WILL HAPPEN IF THERE IS A DRAFT?

It may never happen. Then again, things have been a little dicey lately. The following sequence of events is excerpted from the official U.S. Department of Defense Web site, DefendAmerica.gov.

1. Congress and the president authorize a draft. A crisis occurs which requires more troops than the volunteer military can supply. Congress passes and the President signs legislation which starts a draft.

2. The lottery. A lottery based on birthdays determines the order in which registered men are called up by Selective Service. The first to be called, in a sequence determined by the lottery, will be men whose 20th birthday falls during that year, followed, if needed, by those aged 21, 22, 23, 24 and 25. 18-year-olds and those turning 19 would probably not be drafted.

3. All parts of Selective Service are activated. The Agency activates and orders its State Directors and Reserve Forces Officers to report for duty.

4. Physical, mental, and moral evaluation of registrants. Registrants with low lottery numbers are ordered to report for a physical, mental, and moral evaluation at a Military Entrance Processing Station to determine whether they are fit for military service. Once he is notified of the results of the evaluation, a registrant will be given ten days to file a claim for exemption, postponement, or deferment.

5. Local and appeal boards activated and induction notices sent. Local and Appeal boards will process registrant claims. Those who pass the military evaluation will receive induction orders. An inductee will have 10 days to report to a local Military Entrance Processing Station for induction.

6. First draftees are inducted. According to current plans, Selective Service must deliver the first inductees to the military within 193 days from the onset of a crisis.

Some people simply "forget" to register with Selective Service. The U.S. government does not approve of that tactic and warns: "Young men convicted of failure to register may be fined up to $250,000, imprisoned for up to five years, or both. In addition to being subject to prosecution, failure to register may cause you to permanently forfeit eligibility for certain benefits. **Not registering is a felony.**"

What *really* happens if your son doesn't register? More than five hundred thousand men have done so, and only twenty individuals have been prosecuted, all prior to 1985. However, this doesn't mean the government won't suddenly decide to ramp up prosecutions. There is another drawback to failing to register: Your son won't be eligible for federal student financial aid, training, or employment. Some states withhold their student financial aid as well; some forbid nonregistrants from attending state colleges and universities; some won't let nonregistrants get a driver's license.

Men who fail to register within thirty days of their eighteenth birthday are subject to prosecution. Under the current policy, your son won't be prosecuted unless the Justice Department sends you a "final warning" letter. He may get a similar letter from the IRS or Selective Service System. If he receives such a letter, it's time to visit a draft counselor or an attorney who specializes in draft law.

 ODD ARCHIVES ———————————

It is unknowable how long [the Iraq] conflict will last. It could last six days, six weeks. I doubt six months.
— U.S. Secretary of Defense Donald Rumsfeld, February 7, 2003

HOW CAN MY CHILD SET THE STAGE FOR BEING A CONSCIENTIOUS OBJECTOR?

It may seem calculating, but if he does not "set the stage" your son may have a very difficult time convincing a draft board that he sincerely opposes war. The conscientious objector must prove sincerity, and that means establishing a paper trail.

A crucial element of the current law is that only men who

object to "participation in war in any form" can qualify as conscientious objectors (COs). Your son cannot say that he objects to fighting in certain conflicts but would agree to fight in others. It's all or nothing. However, he is not required to declare how he would have behaved in past wars, for instance in World War II. (Draft board members might ask him a question like that at his hearing, but he doesn't have to answer it.)

Conscientious-objector status used to depend on one's membership in a pacifist religious group, such as the Quakers. That is no longer the case. In 1970, the Supreme Court reinterpreted the section of the Military Selective Service Acts that states that conscientious objectors must oppose participation in war in any form "by reason of religious training and belief." The justices ruled that "religious training and belief" had to include moral and ethical beliefs that were not necessarily part of an organized religion. However, the law also states that objecting to war because of "a merely personal moral code" is not sufficient to qualify someone as a CO. The bottom line is that membership in a pacifist group (religious or otherwise) for a number of years prior to being drafted may help your child's case, but it is not enough to ensure him CO status. He has to prove that he deeply believes in the principles of nonviolence and has for a long time, not just since he got his draft notice.

So back to the paper trail. Let's start with the registration process itself and then discuss the evidence that may support your child's opposition to war. When your son goes to the post office to register with Selective Service, he should write the following in black ink across the registration card:

"I am a conscientious objector to war in any form." He should ask for a second card, do the same thing, write "duplicate" on it, and ask the clerk to stamp both cards. He should keep the duplicate, both as proof that he has registered with Selective Service (he may need it when he applies for financial aid) and as proof that he has identified himself as a CO. This isn't for legal purposes but to establish his philosophical position right from the beginning. If the post-office clerk won't give him a duplicate registration card, he should photocopy the card, fold it in half, tape it closed, and mail the photocopy to himself. That way he will have post-marked proof of registration. The post office does not supply a receipt.

When filling out the registration card, your son should list a reliable return address. If he ever got called to serve, the amount of time the draft notice spends in the mail is taken out of the ten days he is allotted to request a deferment or exemption. (See pages 227 and 228 for a list of these.)

The body of evidence regarding your child's beliefs and sincerity should be collected in a file and sent to the Center on Conscience & War (centeronconscience.org) to be archived. He should also keep a copy for himself. The file should include a statement of beliefs written by your son describing how he came to be a conscientious objector. This statement should mention: membership in any group or congregation that has nonviolence as a core principle; a list of books, films, philosophical statements, pieces of music, and so forth that influenced his ideas about war and killing; personal experiences; pertinent events he has attended throughout his life; nonviolent or pacifist organizations he has supported or belonged to; photos or videos of himself at events that pertained to peace or nonviolence; and anything else that could be used to bolster his claim. The file should also contain letters from three individuals who will attest to your son's beliefs. People who have known him a long time and are not related to him, such as teachers, coaches, and clergy people, are excellent references.

With this paper trail as a foundation, your son or daughter will be in the strongest position to request a CO deferment. There are also deferments and exemptions other than Conscientious Objector that your child may qualify for. He can't apply for them now, but if he were to be drafted, he would need to apply within ten days of receiving his draft notice. (The ten-day rule applies for CO requests as well.) An excellent Web site, abilitymaine.org, offers the following list of deferments and exemptions.

- Student postponements are available for students in high schools, vocational schools, etc., who are age 20 or under.
- College students can receive postponements until the end of the term, or of the year for seniors. Ministry students are exempt if in accepted divinity schools.
- Physical Exemptions: Standards are complex and fill 23 pages of government manuals, but many are as common as hay fever, flat feet, or being overweight. Draft counselors have the whole list and can help you determine which you may qualify for.

- Mental exemptions: Standards are also complex, but you do not have to be mentally ill to qualify. Some "mental problems" for the army are no problem in civilian life.
- Hardship deferments are available if your absence would be a financial, emotional, or physical problem for your wife, children, parents, grandparents, sisters, or brothers.

You may also qualify for exemption or deferment if:

- Your father, mother, sister, or brother died from service-related injuries or illness during or after their service;
- You are a full-time minister (ordained or unordained), or a ministry student;
- You are a citizen of another country;
- You have been in the service or in certain other government agencies; or
- You do not meet moral standards. [The vague wording probably refers to sexual orientation—presumably assessed without asking.]

WHATEVER HAPPENED TO TELECOMMUTING?

Back in the days when the Web was breathlessly referred to as the Information Superhighway, we all thought it was only a matter of two or three years before our employers would allow—nay, urge—us to work from home a few days a week. Many people foresaw a time when they would come in to the office only once or twice a month. It seemed that so many things could be improved by telecommuting: congested freeways, air pollution, hours wasted at the water cooler, the cost of office space, employee morale. In that scenario, workers would occasionally gather at local telecommuting centers to rub shoulders with their comrades or take part in the video conferences that would replace face-to-face meetings. Best of all, productivity would soar, because the telecommuters would be less stressed and more willing to work long hours in order to meet their deadlines and maintain their stay-at-home privileges.

Sure enough, most of the positive predictions about telecommuting came true—for people lucky enough to be offered the option. Several companies, including Dow Chemical, JD Edwards, and American Express, report that their teleworkers increase their productivity anywhere from 7 to 45 percent, with most improving by about 25 percent. (Not surprisingly, a 2005 survey by America Online and salary.com reported that the average office worker wastes about 25 percent of the day gabbing with coworkers and surfing the Net.) Most employees love the flexibility of telecommuting and do indeed put in extra hours if necessary to meet their goals. Because they are happier, their rate of absenteeism is lower than that of nine-to-fivers. While there are a few slackers who don't get the job done, the research overwhelmingly suggests that the pros of allowing employees to telecommute far outweigh the cons.

Why, then, don't more organizations encourage telecommuting? The primary reasons are the same ones that have dogged the movement from the beginning. Employers tend to distrust their workers. They are accustomed to doing things the old-fashioned way. With the exception of IT businesses and those that rely on salespeople working in the field (such as insurance companies), many organizations have balked at telecommuting because managers don't want to lose control of their employees. Some fear that if they let a few people telecommute, everyone will want to do it, and then— kablooey! No more workforce, just a few hapless managers prowling the halls with no one to manage except the custodial staff.

However, it turns out that not everyone wants to telecommute anyway. For some, the isolation is too distressing, even if they are only telecommuting part-time. They miss the meetings, group lunches, and general camaraderie of the office. Another problem arises when the job market gets tight: Telecommuters become nervous about not putting in enough face time to cement relationships with their boss and coworkers. Being out of the loop makes them feel more vulnerable to layoffs.

Whether or not individual employees end up telecommuting, there is little doubt that people want the option. Soaring gasoline prices provide a compelling and socially responsible reason to stay off the roads one or two days a week. The telecommuting movement may grow in fits and starts, but it is definitely here to stay. As of 2006, 12 million people were telecommuting full-time in the United States, and another 10 million did so at least one day a week.

 ODD ARCHIVES

Women need protection from work that is not appropriate for the feminine sex, such as driving a truck, construction work, road work, or anything greasy or masculine. Some types of office work are inappropriate, such as executive jobs, management positions, police work, or top political posts."

—*Fascinating Womanhood,* by Helen Andelin, 1963 (updated 1992)

HOW CAN I CONVINCE MY BOSS TO LET ME TELECOMMUTE?

Most telecommuting jobs begin as regular nine-to-five positions. Either the company launches a telecommuting program, or enterprising employees broach the topic themselves. Baby boomers with a track record of high performance are in the ideal position to bring the concept to the table, because most managers would rather hold on to a reliable employee than be forced to hire and train someone new.

The first step in your telecommuting strategy is to make sure you have the space and equipment you'll need for a home office. Most people already have a computer, but it may need software from work or additional capabilities. Next, determine which elements of your job could be handled from home. Typical tasks include sales and customer-service calls, data input, writing, research, reading, and any activity that involves sitting at a computer. At workathomesuccess.com, you'll find a Work at Home Proposal that will help you out-line your plan and provide your boss with the information he or she needs to feel comfortable with the idea. Telework mavens agree that a two-pronged approach—in-person pre-sentation coupled with a written proposal—is the most likely to succeed.

A prudent tactic is to ask to telecommute one day a week for a three-month trial period, with regular meetings scheduled to report on your productivity. Once you have shown the boss how painless it is, you may be able to work from home two or three days a week. (The average telecommute is two days, according to the International Telework Association.) Assuming that your job is suitable for telecommuting, your biggest challenge will be to con-vince your employer that it will pose no threat to anyone and will save money. Do not say, "The company will bene-fit because I will be less stressed. A happy worker is a pro-ductive worker." That is true but irrelevant. Your mental well-being and gasoline bills generally do not matter to the powers that be.

Instead, begin by assuring your boss that the work you do at home will be measurable—a project with specific milestones, a certain number of phone calls, a weekly or monthly report. The more easily your productivity can be measured, the more comfortable your boss will be about let-ting you work from home.

You will also want to explain why your performance will actually improve on the days you're telecommuting. You could mention that you will have fewer distractions, a quieter environment, or better access to certain clients. It is definitely worth brainstorming to come up with specific reasons that you'll be extra productive on your telecommuting days.

Remind your employer of any projects you've been involved with that required self-discipline, initiative, or other traits that are desirable in a telecommuter. Assure him or her that you will be at the office for all important meetings. Finally, think about other ways that your being home for a day might benefit the organization. For instance, you could offer to telecommute on a day when your absence will free up a desk for a part-time employee.

There is a chance your employer will be less than enthusiastic about this entirely sensible plan. Here are the most common objections to telecommuting, along with some useful comebacks.

"If I let you telecommute, everyone will want to do it." It's true that most employees value the option of telecommuting. In fact, in a survey of 1,400 CFOs conducted by Robert Half International, 46 percent rated telecommuting second to salary in attracting employees. Thirty-three percent said it was *more* important than salary. Telecommuting enhances a company's reputation as well as its productivity. Why not set up a pilot program and see if it works?

"Our company doesn't offer telecommuting." Go to your meeting equipped with information about other similar businesses, preferably in your area, that do let employees telecommute. If it's a competitor, so much the better. Your employer may not want to be the first to offer telecommuting, but he or she probably won't want to be the last, either. A phone call to the human resources departments of these companies should give you the facts you need. You could also mention that according to Mercer Human Resources, as of 2005, 44 percent of companies in the United States offered telecommuting options.

"Your coworkers need access to you." With instant messaging, e-mail, and cell phones, they will be able to reach you anytime, anywhere. Since the advent of instant messaging, many employees don't see each other face-to-face all that often even when they're at the office. This is a plus for productivity, because fewer in-person chats means less gossip and wasted time.

"We can't afford to set up a workstation for you at home." Ask how much it would cost. It may only be the price of a laptop. If you have done your homework and already researched the cost, you can offer your own estimate. Number crunchers at Nortel Networks found that the cost of setting up a home workstation was recouped in the first year if at least 3.5 absent days were avoided—that is, days when a worker would have had to stay home with a sick child or take time off for a doctor's appointment.

"No." If the boss simply refuses to discuss it, leave your proposal with him or her. You can try again in a few months, perhaps when a project that is especially well-suited to telecommuting lands on your desk.

ODD ARCHIVES

By 2000, the machines will be producing so much that
everyone in the U.S. will, in effect, be independently wealthy.
—*Time,* 1966

WHAT ARE THE BEST FOREIGN COUNTRIES TO LIVE IN?

Expatriate is a glamorous word. Most people associate it with
smoky cafes and impossible dreams. But for those bold
enough to try it, moving offshore can render the impossible—
such as retirement—achievable. If you don't feel like com-
muting until you're seventy, becoming an expat might be the
most practical decision you could make.

For nearly three decades, *International Living* magazine has
tracked the lives and fortunes of Americans living outside the
United States. According to publisher Kathleen Peddicord, the
magazine's goal is to help its readers "discover places that are
undervalued . . . under appreciated . . . under-developed . . .
places that the masses have yet to find. And then to help you
understand how you can take advantage of the opportunities
these places offer—to improve your quality of life . . . to
lower your cost of living . . . and to invest for profitable
return—before the rest of the world catches on." To that end,
International Living compiles an annual list of the best places
for Americans to relocate. The criteria range from cost of living and quality of health care to cultural activities and climate.
In 2006, the top ten countries for expats of all ages were:

Argentina	Ireland
Croatia	Italy
Ecuador	Malta
France	Mexico
Honduras	New Zealand

The top ten countries for retirees were:

Panama	France
Malta	Romania
New Zealand	Argentina
Uruguay	Malaysia
Mexico	Ecuador

The magazine's Web site, internationalliving.com, offers a smorgasbord of information on dozens of countries. It has resources both for retirees and for people who want to work or start businesses offshore. Replete with forums, photos, links, and twenty-eight years' worth of accumulated knowledge, it's a good place to test the foreign waters.

 EXPERT INPUT ————————————

Suzan Haskins
Editor and Writer, *International Living* magazine

When Suzan Haskins and her husband were in their midforties, they left Omaha, Nebraska, and moved to Latin America. They have lived in Ecuador, Mexico, Panama, and Nicaragua.

How and why did you decide to move outside the United States?

My husband and I had an advertising and marketing agency, and by 1999 it had gotten to the point where we had to hire more people. We really didn't want to do that; we didn't want to be any more responsible than we already were. So we started thinking about making a life change and where we might want to move. We narrowed our choices down to Latin America because we had traveled there extensively.

We were both degreed journalists, so I got in touch with *International Living* and asked if they had any opportunities for us. Lo and behold, they needed people in Quito, Ecuador. Within a couple of months we had put our house up for sale, sold our cars and trucks, put the things that meant something to us in storage, and moved to Ecuador.

What was it like to make this change? It sounds as if you were an experienced traveler already.

I was; my husband wasn't. He was born and raised in Omaha and lived there his entire life. He had the same friends he'd had since high school, so for him, at age 47, it was a bit more of a change. I had lived in Omaha for twenty years, so I had some close friends there as well.

It's always a culture shock, no matter where you go or what you do, especially if you're moving to a foreign country. Like everyone who does this, we had that initial feeling of, "Oh, my God. What have we done?" The hardest thing for both of us was missing our friends—not being able to pick up the phone and say, "Come on over for dinner," and know that they would drop by in whatever they happened to be wearing and eat whatever we happened to be serving. Latin America is a much more formal society than the United States. People dress to go to dinner; they go to dinner late. When you invite someone to your home, there are different social expectations. My husband had never owned a tuxedo, and the first year we were in Ecuador we were invited to three formal balls where he had to wear a tuxedo.

When you made friends, was it mostly with other expatriates?
For us, it's both expatriates and local people, because we're not only living here, we're also working.

What are some of the challenges expatriates face when they first arrive?
The language. If you don't speak Spanish, you are definitely at a disadvantage. That doesn't mean you can't function here, it just means your experience will be different. Most of the professionals you come into contact with do speak English.

There's a different business protocol here; this was especially true in Ecuador. Businesses close for two hours during lunchtime; even the banks close. You can't get anything done between one o'clock and three o'clock in the afternoon. Or sometimes it's between two and four, depending on the local custom. In the States, I was used to picking up the phone or going online and doing eight things in the course of a day. To go to the bank in Ecuador we had to physically *go* there—it would require effort on our part. My productivity level went down seriously. Instead of getting eight things done in a day, I might get one thing done.

In the end, does it matter much?
It doesn't matter at all! But that first year, it seemed to matter a lot. It takes time, and it takes realizing that you're going to have to change the way you think. If you can't accept that you're going to change your life—which is what you wanted to do in the first place—then you might as well stay home.

What kinds of people make the move successfully, and what kinds do not?
Couples have a good chance, because you always have someone to lean on and talk to. At the same time, I've seen as many singles as couples succeed at this. If you're a strong type A personality, you're probably going to have more problems, because you're more apt to want things done your way, and this is not your place anymore. You have to acclimatize to the people who live here. I hate it when I hear Americans say, "Why can't these people do it *this* way?" It tells me either that they're new or that they've never accepted the way things are done in this culture.

What kind of stress does this life place on a couple?
By and large, if the couple has a good relationship, they do fine. In the States, if a couple retires and are suddenly around each other all day, they don't really have any new

challenges. They have to decide what they're going to do with their time—play golf, play bridge, do volunteer work, et cetera. When you move offshore, you have more opportunities for new experiences. You're probably learning a new language. You're learning about the community that you live in. You're forcing yourself to learn, and everything is new to both of you. The couples I've seen who have moved here seem to get along really well, because they have this shared agenda.

What about people who aren't in the travel industry like you are—have many of them been able to find work?
I rarely see anyone who's purely retired. Most people come here to Latin America and discover that there are many niches to be filled, many business opportunities. Real estate is a big one. All the baby boomers are looking for retirement communities or expat communities or *non*expat communities. There are opportunities to get into real-estate development with locals who are looking for the expertise we as North Americans bring. They want to know what we're looking for in homes: How should they build the kitchens? The bathrooms?

Then there are all of the other niches that need to be filled. For example, there are no Thai or Indian restaurants here. Some people start a tour company. You can teach English for pay or as a volunteer. You may not know that you have certain skills and expertise, but when you get here and people keep asking your opinion, you realize, "Maybe I do have something to offer." It's really very exciting.

*What general advice would you give midlifers
considering a move to a foreign country?*
If you're thinking about retiring to a place like Latin America, you might be able to do it earlier than you thought you could, because the cost of living here is so much lower. My advice is, just do it. If you decide that you've made a mistake, you can always go home. You'll go home a different person and a better person.

WHAT IS THE FUTURE OF RETIREMENT?

"Traditional retirement has become the exception, not the rule. . . . For a majority of older Americans, retirement is a process, often over many years, and not a single event." So concluded a ten-year study published in 2005 by the U.S. Bureau of Labor Statistics. The economy has shifted, and unless you are wealthy or one of the few remaining recipients of a defined-benefit pension plan (the type that pays a set, guaranteed dollar amount every month for the rest of your life), you will likely have a slow transition to full retirement. However, you will have lots of company: Your equally pension-deprived or ill-prepared boomer friends will be joining you in the transitional job market, working part time at "bridge" jobs that range from the satisfying and lucrative (such as consulting for your previous full-time employer) to the dreary and underpaid. The grouchy seniors who work at my local Staples and Best Buy fall into the latter category, I suspect. I'd be cranky too if I had to spend all day hoisting big-screen TVs for credit-mad thirty-somethings. Of course, all that spending and so little saving is what will propel the youngsters into the service sector themselves when they're 65. It's what passes for the circle of life around here.

It's hard to believe that twenty years ago the talk was all about *early* retirement. Back then, corporations were downsizing and forcing hundreds of thousands of employees to retire before they wanted to (with defined-benefit pension plans, or some version of them, intact). "Forced early retirement, unanticipated and without time to plan, is expected to be especially stressful," wrote William R. Gillanders in the *Journal of Family Practice* (April 1991). "Income falls, radically altering lifestyles. . . . Forced early retirees may be unable to afford medical care. . . . Wrenched suddenly from their jobs, forced early retirees may lose support networks of friends and co-workers."

According to beliefs popular at the time, Gillanders reported, "Retirement implies failure to perform, which reduces self-respect and status, which leads to further withdrawal from social participation, which leads to isolation, illness, and decline in happiness and life satisfaction." To test these theories, he looked at the health of steelworkers ages 50 to 62 who were forced into taking early retirement by widespread mill closings in the late 1970s. After following the retirees for eleven years, he concluded that their health was the same as that of anyone else in their age group, and their self-esteem was A-OK too.

Today, concern about the mental and physical well-being of midlife pensioners seems quaint indeed. Only about one in five public-sector workers has a defined-benefit pension, and the number is decreasing every year. Approximately 45 percent of private-sector full-time employees are not offered any retirement plan at all. Companies don't like defined benefits, in part because, as retirees live longer, the cost goes up. Most people who do have a pension have a 401(k) or other defined-contribution plan, where the employee contributes to company-run portfolios, owns the assets, and assumes the risks inherent in the investment.

Among the companies with defined-benefit plans, many don't have enough assets to cover their retirees' pensions. If the pension funds aren't adequate, the U.S government's Pension Benefit Guaranty Corporation (PBGC) is supposed to step in and pay the benefits. When they do, the amount is often less than the retirees were originally promised. And the PBGC is low on funds itself—$23 billion short as of this writing. A massive pension bill passed in 2006 addressed some of these problems, forcing companies to fund their retirement plans more responsibly and bolstering PBGC's coffers. But the fact remains that cushy defined-benefit plans seem to be on the way out.

My generation has always preferred whistling past the graveyard to planning for the years preceding it. "Pre-retirees have not given much thought to their living and finances in retirement," concluded a 2004 MetLife Mature

Market Institute/AARP survey of 50- to 65-year-olds. Seventy-nine percent of them reported "*little* or *no* concern about whether they will have enough money to live comfortably throughout their retirement years." Sixty percent mistakenly assumed that Medicare would cover their expenses if they needed long-term care. Forty percent had not bothered to create a financial plan so that their savings might last through retirement.

In 2006, AARP again questioned U.S. adults about their plans for the future, this time including those 40 and up. Their responses were similar, with the exception being that more people were worried about retirement than they had been in 2004. Worry hadn't translated into action, however: Of the respondents, 56 percent had not calculated their retirement needs, and 31 percent had not saved a penny for retirement. About half had less than $25,000 in savings and investments, not counting the value of their home. As a group, older workers (age 55 and up) were not any more likely to have savings than those age 40 to 54.

It wouldn't be fair to assume that overspending and willful ignorance were the sole reasons for their empty bank accounts. The rising costs of housing and health care place a financial burden on many families that makes it nearly impossible to save. The workers themselves list the top six reasons for their lack of savings as high everyday expenses, insufficient income, a bad economy, the cost of raising children, health or medical expenses, and lack of financial discipline.

The background stories of the survey respondents reveal what many across the country were, and are, facing in terms of retirement planning. In the previous five years:

- 10 percent of the respondents' employers had eliminated a traditional defined-benefit pension plan;
- 9 percent of employers had frozen or reduced existing traditional pension benefits;
- 15 percent of employers had changed a traditional pension plan into a defined-contribution plan; and
- 44 percent of employers had reduced health-care benefits

According to the study, current retirees derive their income primarily from Social Security, traditional pension benefits, and personal investments. Fifty-eight percent of these retirees listed Social Security as a major source of income. In 2005, the maximum Social Security payment was $1,939 a month for people applying at full retirement age (65 and 6 months for those born in and after 1940; it will gradually increase to 67 for people born in and after 1960). Not everyone gets the maximum, however. Your benefit is based on a formula applied to your previous income. The *average* benefit for a single retiree was $955, and for a married retired couple it was $1,574.

How you fit into the retirement picture depends on the assets you expect to have when you reach retirement age. With reliable pensions becoming more rare, the option of knocking off at 62 and touring wine country for the next thirty years is going to be available to fewer among us. By the same token, not many people *want* to taste wine for thirty years. Yet another AARP survey found that, while the average baby boomer expects to quit his or her full-time job at age 66, about 80 percent of them also expect to keep working at some sort of part-time or bridge job.

Those expectations and how they play out were the subject of a unique study conducted in 2005 by Katherine G. Abraham and Susan G. Houseman for the Upjohn Institute. The dramatic news was how few midlifers who wanted to switch to part-time work were able to do so. At the end of the eight-year survey, only 36 percent had pulled it off. Another 36 percent were working the same number of hours or more, and 27 percent had stopped working altogether.

Of people who claimed they wanted to transition to part-time work, those who held several jobs were most successful at achieving the goal. They simply quit one of their jobs. Other workers negotiated fewer hours with their existing employer. The self-employed could call their own shots. People who attempted to reduce their hours by changing jobs had the least success. The study found that older workers have a difficult time transitioning to a new job: Many have not job-hunted for years and lack connections to outside employers. Some are unwilling to accept less pay and fewer benefits than they enjoyed at their former job. And others are unable or unwilling to learn new skills.

Age discrimination is a problem as well, and it is not going away as quickly as we might like. In May 2007, *Los Angeles Times* writer Jonathan Peterson reported on the trend among older workers to postpone retirement. In addition to the need for income, "the economy's long-term shift toward knowledge-based jobs and away from physical labor is another force that might be increasing the rolls of older workers," he wrote. Yet although it is unquestionably good for the economy when boomers remain on the job (paying taxes as opposed to collecting Social Security checks) companies do not always welcome them, Peterson reported. Researchers at Boston College who interviewed more than four hundred employers found that "many companies were only 'lukewarm' about accommodating older workers who might be willing to stay on the job a few extra years."

Whether for financial reasons, health-insurance benefits, or intellectual and emotional fulfillment, many people will be working into their late sixties and beyond. If you are in your early fifties and are gainfully employed, you're in a good position to start thinking about a transitional job and acquiring the new skills you might need a few years down the line. It's not that old dogs *can't* learn new tricks, it's that sometimes they don't feel like it. And that can make a person cranky.

THE GOOD NEWS

Maybe It's Time to Write That Book

According to a survey of novels that topped the *New York Times* Bestseller List from 1955 to 2004, the average age of the books' authors was 50.5 years. The survey was conducted by Lulu, a company that prints books on demand. They looked at more than 350 authors in order to discover the optimum age to write a best-selling work of fiction. "We suspected that it was higher than many people assume. Unlike scientists or musicians, say, writers tend to mature with age," said Lulu CEO and founder Bob Young, who is 53.

WILL I HAVE TO CHOOSE BETWEEN SUN CITY AND SIN CITY?

When it comes to predicting where the baby boomers will spend their golden years, real-estate developers, social scientists, and other prognosticators are all atwitter. After assuring us for the umpteenth time that we are nothing like our parents, they boldly forecast that we will not want to end up in old-age homes (as if today's seniors do). "Aging in place" is the current lingo for growing old in your own home, and the concept is ground zero for any discussion about retirement housing. By dint of our numbers—80 million over 65 by 2030—boomers have the clout to make aging in place more attainable for everyone, and that is undeniably a good thing.

From a design point of view, aging in place means housing

that can accommodate all types of people, from the spry to the physically disabled. Single-level dwellings, wheelchair accessibility, wide doorways, easy-grip fixtures, and skidproof flooring are only a few of the design elements builders include in new housing geared toward retirees. Smart contractors are currently doing a brisk business retrofitting existing homes to meet these standards, and demand is only going to increase. (If you're handy with tools, there's a part-time job idea. You're guaranteed a steady flow of clients, none of whom will hold it against you that you're not 25.)

From the lifestyle perspective, aging in place means access to all the services you need, even if you can no longer drive. In response to seniors' desire to continue living at home, a grassroots movement called NORCs has developed over the past ten years. NORCs—naturally occurring retirement communities—are neighborhoods or apartment buildings whose senior residents have created a formal or informal support system. The typical NORC is made up of neighbors age 60 and over who moved into the area when they were younger and have literally aged in place. Pooling their money, they arrange for weekly shopping trips and discounted rates for services, such as in-home health care, cleaning, home maintenance, and meal delivery.

There are also a growing number of communities that are officially classified as NORCs and receive a full array of state- or city-funded services that include everything from mental-health counseling to legal and financial planning to cultural outings. New York City has twenty-seven such NORCs. Religious organizations fund NORCs in some cities.

For instance, Eldersource of Greater Indianapolis is run by the Jewish Federation but serves senior citizens of any denomination. Other NORCs are funded by a combination of community organizations, businesses, government agencies, and residents. The National Aging in Place Council (naipc.org) is a clearinghouse for information about NORCs and can point you to services in your area.

Another major force driving the housing decisions of boomers is the fact that many of them will not retire in their sixties. Even if they cash out their houses and move to cheaper digs or smaller towns, many will need to work at least part-time. That limits the number of boomers who can afford to move permanently to a beloved mountain community or seacoast resort, where jobs are scarce. Yet contrary to the stereotype of "snowbirds" migrating south for the winter, most people tend to retire near their former homes anyway, especially if their family lives nearby. Over the past fifty years, the number of retirees who move out of state has been consistently under 5 percent. Five percent of 80 million retirees is still a sizable number, however, and it has fueled a building boom of retirement communities in places such as Nevada, North Carolina, Colorado, and Idaho, as well as the traditional havens of Florida, Arizona, and California. But boomers will have many other choices as well. Here are some emerging trends:

We'll stay put, but with a little help. The NORCs movement mentioned above is leading the push for aging in place. Even if you don't live in a neighborhood with enough seniors to form a NORC, you will still be able to take advantage of services and retrofitting that enable you to live at home for as long as possible. The National Association of Home Builders now offers a CAPS (Certified Aging-in-Place Specialist) designation, and the group estimates that within a few years aging-in-place renovations may bring in $20 billion worth of business annually. The sheer number of aging boomers will force government and private agencies to provide more in-home services, according to some experts, who anticipate that there will not be enough assisted-living facilities to house everyone who needs day-to-day help.

We'll move to a college town. University-linked retirement communities (ULRCs) offer senior housing on or near college campuses. There are about sixty of these around the country as of this writing, and chances are that many more will be built in the coming years. The attraction for retirees is obvious: Campus life provides intellectual stimulation, entertainment, and sophistication in a small-town setting. ULRCs are a terrific source of revenue for the campuses, which often have plenty of spare land on which to build housing. The seniors who live in the communities are a rich source of income, spending money on classes, activities, fundraising, and taxes, not to mention expenses such as food and clothing. They have no young children, so they don't affect the school system. It's a win-win for the colleges and the seniors.

ULRCs are built either as for-profit developments or as nonprofits. The for-profit housing can be as upscale as the most exclusive country club. At Traditions, a golf resort catering to Texas A&M alums of all ages and located about two miles from campus, the entrance fees start in the six figures and can reach nearly two million dollars, with monthly fees up to five thousand dollars. (Ninety percent of the entrance fees are refundable if residents leave the community.)

For seniors who don't have a spare couple of million to plunk down, nonprofit developers offer an appealing alternative. To see just how appealing, check out the properties at Kendal Corporation's Web site (kendal.org).

We'll move to a retirement-friendly city. The Sun Belt stranglehold on retirement destinations is over. Numerous organizations have published lists of the best places to retire, rating attributes such as cost of living, climate, crime, services, employment, entertainment, and transportation. While cities in Arizona, Florida, and California are always represented, they have plenty of competition. MyThirdLife .com put together a list of eleven favorites, the criterion being that each town had appeared on two other "best" lists. In alphabetical order, they are:

Bellingham, WA	Prescott, AZ
Bend, OR	San Diego, CA
Chapel Hill, NC	Santa Fe, NM
Charlottesville, VA	Sarasota, FL
Fort Collins, CO	Tucson, AZ
Fort Myers, FL	

We'll seek the company of others like ourselves. Age-restricted retirement communities feel comforting to some people, claustrophobic to others. Now, for the first time, there are communities designed for groups that have been excluded from the conventional developments. Rainbow Vision condominiums in Santa Fe and Palm Springs cater to gay and lesbian seniors, as do about twenty other retirement communities across the United States, with more planned. Other developments target Asian-Americans, military veterans, and golfers. ElderSpirit, located in the Appalachian Mountains, was founded by a group of former nuns and welcomes seniors of all denominations who yearn to develop their spirituality.

We'll move to traditional retirement communities, only we'll call them "active adult" communities. Here's the big question that has bedeviled retirement developers for the past ten years: Will baby boomers go for the same thing their parents did? Will they be interested in age-restricted communities that focus on leisure and are situated off the beaten path? At this point the answer seems to be yes, some will. The key to luring us, apparently, is to stress how active the lifestyle will be. Del Webb, the retirement industry's Goliath, took this approach to market Corte Bella, its first "active adult community for people 55 or better." The company's Web site coos about its "state-of-the-art fitness centers and exquisite golf courses . . . a variety of classes and clubs ranging from ceramics to computers to personal investing . . . a lifestyle that allows you to set your own course." Corte Bella has "everything expected in an elite golf community except the attitude," declares the ad copy. It may look like your father's retirement village, but it's not, because . . . um . . . the furniture is midcentury modern.

We'll move into cohousing communities. Imagine a condominium complex with a soul, green architecture, and residents you actually like. The sophisticated distant cousin of the commune, cohousing is quite possibly the wave of the future. Read more about it in the next section.

An interesting observation was made by Mike Baumayr, head of Del Webb's primary ad agency for more than fifteen years. "A housing product means a lot less to boomers than the community it's in," he told David B. Wolfe, founder of agelessmarketing.com. Wolfe agreed: "Few people ascend to new levels of luxury in retirement. 'Luxury' is a materialistic value that most people in their sixties and older . . . don't find all that engaging. It's the community that they want to be engaging. That's not just a boomer thing. It has always been the case."

As we slowly edge toward retirement age, midlifers of all income brackets have an advantage our parents did not. There are so many of us that, if we start voting now on issues that will affect us ten or fifteen years down the line, we have a good chance of being able to live out our lives in relative comfort, in a community that feels like home.

WHAT IS COHOUSING?

It is not a commune, although the "c" word may spring to mind when you first encounter the concept. The most striking difference between a commune and cohousing is that cohousing is meticulously planned and funded by the residents, usually in concert with a developer. Residents' benefits and responsibilities are spelled out in a written agreement, and conflict resolution procedures are outlined down to the last detail. So banish the memory of Peter Fonda in *Easy*

Rider touring a dusty collection of tents on a godforsaken slab of desert ("They're gonna make it, man."). It's not like that, not when everyone has paid hard-earned cash to develop the community.

Cohousing, which originated in Denmark in the 1970s, was introduced to the United States in 1988 when architects Kathryn McCamant and Charles Durrett published their seminal book on the topic, *Cohousing: A Contemporary Approach to Housing Ourselves* (Ten Speed Press, 1993). In it they gave voice to a growing anxiety among baby boomers, and they proposed a solution: "Things that people once took for granted—family, community, a sense of belonging now must be actively sought out. . . . The cohousing concept reestablishes many of the advantages of traditional villages within the context of late-twentieth-century life." Twenty years later, more than two hundred cohousing communities are thriving in the United States.

The first question most people ask about cohousing is, "Will I have my own kitchen?" The answer is yes. However, a big draw for many residents is that meals are served from two to five times a week in the "common house." Dining there is voluntary and residents pay for meals, which typically cost around $2.50 to $3.75. Every adult must occasionally help prepare a meal or clean up afterward; depending on the size of the community, residents usually pull kitchen duty once every four or five weeks.

According to the Cohousing Association of the United States, six features are common to all cohousing communities:

Participatory process. Future residents take part in the planning of the community, along with a developer.

Neighborhood design. The concept of community is a top priority of the physical layout. This most often results in homes that are situated near one another; for instance, across a common courtyard or pedestrian walkway. Contact with neighbors is encouraged by design elements such as front porches and common parks. Cars typically access property from the rear, enhancing the people-focused feel of the neighborhood.

Common facilities. Each cohousing community has a common house that usually includes a kitchen, dining area, sitting area, children's play area, and laundry. Many communities also have extras such as an exercise room, library, workshop, craft room, and a guest room or two for visitors. Depending on whether the community is in an urban setting or a more rural location, it may have a small common outdoor area or many acres of shared open space.

Resident management. Residents share the management of the community and the tasks of maintaining it, unless they all agree to hire someone for a specific job.

Nonhierarchical structure and decision making. In the management of the community, residents volunteer for tasks that reflect their interests and skills. Most cohousing groups make all their decisions by consensus and hold a vote only if an issue becomes contentious.

No shared economy. The community is not a source of income for its members. Different communities have different rules in regards to selling one's residence. Most cohousing communities are financially structured like condominiums: Residents jointly own common property and facilities and are the sole owners of their individual homes. If the property value has increased when they sell their home, they keep the profit. If it loses value, they absorb the loss.

The social and emotional needs that cohousing tries to meet were summed up by Mark Fenster in a 1999 article for the *Journal of Land Use & Environmental Law:* "The cohousing movement explicitly attempts to reject the classic isolationism and ideological homogeneity of the American commune, the single family home's private enclave within wasteful suburban sprawl, and the middle class urban neighborhood that is only drawn together through shared fear of crime and random violence." It is an idealistic endeavor that may be especially challenging for Americans, raised as we are to guard our privacy, property, and individual rights. Reining in our natural impulse to have everything our own way sometimes proves more difficult than residents imagine when they are planning their community. And being a stone's throw from all those neighbors is wonderful until someone marries a cranky loudmouth, or a cute 6-year-old grows into a rock-blasting teenager. But that can happen in any neighborhood, and cohousing communities have the advantage of written procedures already in place to deal with such bumps in the road.

A virtual tour of cohousing communities in the United States reveals many that are quite lovely. Green architecture is encouraged, landscaping is often lush, and the human scale of the developments will warm the heart of many an urban or suburban dweller. Young families seem to make up the majority of residents, but all types are usually welcome, from singles to single parents to midlifers and older folks.

The cost of cohousing is generally a bit higher than that of town homes or condominiums, because the common facilities are more extensive and the green design features tend to be more costly (although they may pay off in the long run). The communities are usually safer than a typical neighborhood for obvious reasons: Everyone knows one another and keeps an eye out for people who don't belong.

If your curiosity is piqued, visit the Cohousing Association's Web site, cohousing.org, for a wealth of information, photos, and links.

 EXPERT INPUT

Ann Zabaldo, Cohousing Pioneer

Ann Zabaldo has been part of the cohousing movement in the United States since the early 1990s. She is a principal in Cohousing Collaborative, a development company that works with clients to create cohousing communities. Ann lives in Takoma Village, a community she helped develop near Washington, D.C.

What is the age range of the residents in Takoma Village?
We have a new baby not quite a year old, and our eldest member is 86. In 2000, when the community first opened,

most of the residents were between 30 and 50. There were also a number of seniors. Right now, we're raising twenty-two children here. Out of sixty-six adults in the community, twenty-four are between the ages of 45 and 65.

How would midlifers benefit from living in a cohousing community?
For midlife single men and women, cohousing can provide a sense of belonging, like having an extended family. This can be very healing for those midlifers exiting a marriage. For midliters raising a family, having a community of people you trust with your children is a godsend. For single women, it's especially good. This may be a stereotype, but I think women have a propensity for teamwork. They're less likely to live alone, and cohousing provides a balance. You own your own home, and you have a community.

Take me, for instance. I had been living in a group house for five years. It was a mixed group of men and women, and I was thinking, "OK, this is interesting, but isn't there another step after this? If you're not going to get married, what's next?" Someone suggested I read the book *Cohousing: A Contemporary Approach to Housing Ourselves.* I opened the book up, I read a couple of paragraphs, and I closed the book. I said to myself, *This is the road to peace.* It's the old Gandhi concept: Be the change you want to see. If we can figure out who empties the trash, maybe we have a shot a doing something in the Middle East.

I saw immediately that cohousing could address social ills like latchkey kids. I was a latchkey kid, and we don't have latchkey children here at Takoma. Cohousing is how we can make housing fit our needs for community, instead of trying to make our community fit within the four walls of our house.

How do the various ages in the community affect the dynamics?
Certainly older members have more life experience. They're helpful to the people who have new babies or who are adopting children. We've had five or six adoptions here. We have three single men who adopted children; that's pretty unusual. We also have some single mothers.

Do the adoption agencies see the community as a plus?
Absolutely. They come and do a home visit, and the prospective parents point to the entire community and say, "This is my home." The social workers love us.

How does the reality of living in Takoma Village compare to what you imagined during the development stage?
By the time I moved in to Takoma, I had already had a lot of experience in the cohousing movement. I was on the board of directors of the Cohousing Association of the United States, I was the president of the organization, and I had already founded Mid-Atlantic Cohousing, so my dream for how this was going to be was huge. The bar was really high. All I can tell you is, seven years into this, it has far exceeded every expectation that I had. I'm like a kid in a candy shop.

I'm not saying there haven't been problems. We have

fights, we have fallouts. Just this past year, we had a big set-to in the community. It involved e-mail, and how people were expressing themselves. Some residents thought the e-mails were too harsh and were outraged; other people had no problems with the e-mails. People have different tolerances. One of the outcomes of that conflict was that we started a practice group in nonviolent communication to learn how to communicate our needs to each other. Over the past seven years there have been other conflicts, and for those we had a couple of residents who were willing to act as mediators. It was pretty informal.

What are the main challenges of living in a cohousing community?
At the last big cohousing conference, I heard four main issues being discussed: how to finance new cohousing projects, how to divide up the work, how to decide on community meals, and resolving conflicts in the community.

What are shared meals like at Takoma Village?
You can have an expectation concerning meals when people come into a community, but you can't require them to participate. It's different from community to community. We don't have many set meals here. We have one every Monday, we have a potluck dinner on the full moon (or around then), and we have another potluck called Dinner at Eight. And then we have brunches, parties, barbecues, and a whole bunch of other stuff like that. But some communities eat together five times a week.

Do most of the people who live in Takoma Village have previous experience with shared living?
Other than college or university living, I would say no.

How do they deal with the "communal" aspect of cohousing?
We're technically a condominium; the cohousing part of it is a lifestyle choice. So even if we weren't a cohousing community, there would be property and facilities that belong to the condominium as a whole. We had to learn what kinds of things we could do on our own and what had to pass an architectural review. You can't just paint your door any color you want. It has to go through the homeowners' association. We're located in a historic district, so the rules are more strict than they might be somewhere else.

Management of the community is done through three teams: administrative, community, and facilities. Administrative deals with legal and financial issues; community deals with everything that affects the social life of the community, from births to deaths, meals, holidays, and so forth; and facilities deals with the physical plant, the bricks and mortar.

Here's the difference between us and a condominium. We had a person who installed a doorbell at her front door, not realizing that you can't drill through the envelope of the building. In a condominium, the board would fine the resident. Instead, the facilities team simply advised her, "You know what? You can't do that." If someone is noisy in a condominium, you complain to the management. Here, I go knock on the door.

In a condominium, you have a board that makes the decisions about the daily running of the community. At Takoma, we make the daily decisions as a group, and that makes all the difference in the world. For me, a real test of community is if you can go out your front door and still feel as if you own everything. It's not just your unit. It's your community.

WHAT ARE SOME DECENT ALTERNATIVES TO THE WORDS GRANDMA AND GRANDPA?

If you're delighted with the job description but can't stomach the title, there are plenty of charming alternatives. The list below is culled from languages across the globe.

Grandma	Grandpa	Origin
Abuelita, Ita, Ala, Nana,	Abuelito, Ito, Oto,	Spanish (Latin America)
Avia	Avi	Catalan (Spain)
Avoa	Avo	Galician (Spain)
Baba, Baka	Deda or Deka	Serbian
Bibi	Babu	Swahili (Tanzania)
Bomma	Bompa	Flemish
Bubbe	Zeydeh	Yiddish
Jeeda	Jaddee	Berber

Grandma	Grandpa	Origin
Lola	Lolo	Filipino (Tagalog)
Mamaia	Tataia	Romanian
Nenek	Datuk	Malay
Nonna	Nonno	Italian
Oma	Opa	Dutch
Omi	Opi	German
Savta	Saba	Hebrew
Sitto, Taataa	Siido	Arabic (Persian Gulf)
Yaya, Nona	Papou	Greek

A "Yahoo Answers" search for alternative grandparent names turned up a forum with the usual English-language varieties: Nana, Pops, Grams, and so forth. But there were two unique entries:

"Grumpy and Frumpy."

"Acerbic old b-a-s-t-a-r-d-s with nothing else left to do in their lives but moan moan moan!!"

SELECTED BIBLIOGRAPHY

AARP (American Association for Retired Persons). "Long Term
Care Insurance." 1995–2007. http://aaa.aarp.org/money/
financial_planning/sessionfive/longterm_care_insurance
.html.

AARP (American Association for Retired Persons). "Reverse
Mortgages." 1995–2007. http://www.aarp.org/money/
revmort/.

Abraham, Katherine G., and Susan N. Houseman. "Work and
Retirement Among Older Americans." In *Reinventing the
Retirement Paradigm,* Robert L. Clark and Olivia S. Mitchell,
eds. New York: Oxford University Press, 2005.

Akbar, Arifa. "Middle-Aged Men Winners in the Bedroom." *New
Zealand Herald,* Feb. 22, 2006.

Alexander, Richard, ed. "Avoiding Fraud When Buying Long
Term Care Insurance: A Guide for Consumers and Their
Families." 1994–2007. http://consumerlawpage.com/article/
insurance.shtml.

Amatenstein, Sherry. "What Men Want at 20, 30, and 40."
iVillage. http://love.ivillage.com/lnsunderstandmen/
whathewants/0,,doyenne_813p,00.html.

American Academy of Periodontology. "Small Bacteria—Big
Impact." Apr. 10, 2007. http://www.perio.org/consumer/
perio-systemic.htm.

American Bar Association, Division for Public Education. "The
Probate Process." July 15, 2007. http://www.abanet.org/
publiced/practical/probate.html.

American Heart Association. "Alcohol, Wine and Cardiovascular Disease." 2005. http://www.americanheart.org/presenter.jhtml ?identifier=4422.

American Society for Aesthetic Plastic Surgery. "Cosmetic Surgery Quick Facts: 2005 ASAPS Statistics." 2005. http:// www.surgery.org/press/procedurefacts-asqf.php.

"Another Plus for Red Wine." Cortlandt Forum, Nov. 2004.

Associated Press. "Beer and an Eyebrow Wax? Male Salons Take Off." Dec. 13, 2005. http://www.msnbc.msn.com/id/ 10454245/.

Barclay, Laurie. "Midlife Physical Activity May Be Linked to Reduced Rate of Dementia and Alzheimer's Disease." Medscape Today, Oct. 7, 2005.

BBC News. "MP3 Users Hearing Damage Warning." Aug. 18, 2005. http://news.bbc.co.uk/2/hi/health/4162028.stm.

Berry, Michael. "The Physiology of Taste." http://www.sff.net/ people/mberry/taste.htm.

Bilger, Burkhard. "The Power of Hair." New Yorker, Jan. 9, 2006.

Blaum, Paul. "Don't Sweat Creaking Joints Until They Hurt." Penn State Sports Medicine Newsletter, June 8, 1998. http:// www.psu.edu/ur/NEWS/news/sportsmed.jun98.html.

Bode, Nicole. "Put On a Happy Face." Psychology Today, Jan.–Feb. 2001.

Bozi, Vincent. "Body Talk—Research on What Body Type the Opposite Sex Finds Attractive." Psychology Today, Sept. 1985.

Cahill, Kevin E. "Are Traditional Retirements a Thing of the Past?" U.S. Bureau of Labor Statistics, Working Paper 384, Sept. 2005.

Carillo, Catherine. "The Nose Knows . . . and Remembers!" The Smell & Taste Treatment and Research Foundation. http:// www.scienceofsmell.com/scienceofsmell/index.cfm ?action=noseknows.

Caring Medical. "Fallen Arches or Flatfoot." http://www.caring medical.com/conditions/Fallen_Arches_or_Flatfoot.htm.

CBG Law Group. "The New Bankruptcy Law." 2007. http://
  bankruptcy.findlaw.com/new-bankruptcy-law/.
Center on Conscience & War. "Conscientious Objectors and
  Draft Registration." http://peace.mennolink.org/articles/co_
  advice.html.
Claiborne, Ray C. "Genes and Baldness." New York Times, Sept.
  14, 2004.
Clark, Nancy. "Weight and Menopause." American Fitness,
  March–April 2002.
Clark, Sarah. "Boomtown." Military Officers Association of
  America. http://www.moaa.org/MilitaryOfficer/Archive/2006
  .html.
Clements, Jonathan. "Protecting Your Finances from Your
  Family's Mistakes." Pittsburgh Post-Gazette, Feb. 15, 2006.
CMS/Centers for Medicare and Medicaid Services. "Medicaid."
  Apr. 25, 2006. http://www.cms.hhs.gov/home/medicaid.asp.
Cochran, Sarah, and Tyler Grove. "Medicaid Law: An Overview."
  June 16, 2007. Cornell University Law School. http://www
  .law.cornell.edu/wex/index.php/Medicaid.
Cohousing Association of the United States, The. "What Is
  Cohousing?" http://www.cohousing.org/overview.aspx.
Cole, Kristen. "Whisking Up a Memory with a Whiff." George
  Street Journal. http://www.brown.edu/Administration/George_
  Street_Journal/vol25/25GSJ05a.html.
College Board. "Trends in College Pricing." 2006. http://www
  .collegeboard.com/prod_downloads/press/cost06/trends_
  colege_pricing_06.pdf.
Cook, Bridget. "Wagons Ho!" 2005. Specialty Travel. http://
  specialtytravel.com/stories/stories.cgi?id=15741.
Crawford, Steve. "About Disability Insurance." 2001. http://www
  .about-disability-insurance.com.
Dance with Shadows. "High-end Luxury RVs Can Be Owned by
  Many Together Now." http://www.dancewithshadows.com/
  auto/high-end-luxury-coach.asp.

Davies, Curt. "2005 Travel & Adventure Report." *AARP—The Magazine*. http://www.aarp.org/research/family/travel/boomer _travel.html

Davis, Lisa Nachmias. "What If I Gave It All Away?" Sharing Law. Oct. 18, 2006. http://www.sharinglaw.net/elder/medicaid.htm.

Dawson, James S. "Relationship Between Smoking and Wrinkles Clarified." http://www.studentbmmj.com/back_issues/0501/news/136b.hml.

DentalPlans.com. "Dental Insurance vs. Discount Dental Plans." 1999–2007. http://www.dentalplans.com/moreinfo/plansvsinsurance.asp.

"Determining Biological Age." *Scientific American*, May 13, 2002. http://www.sciam.com/article.cfm?articleID=000BAAA8-3E43-1CE5-93F6809EC5880000.

Deveny, Kathleen. "We're Not in the Mood." *Newsweek*, June 30, 2003.

Drouin, Rachel. "What Are Allergies?" 2005. Women's Web. http://www.womensweb.ca/health/allergies (Feb. 10, 2006).

Dubin, Arlene G. *Prenups for Lovers*. New York: Villard, 2001.

Easterbrook, Gregg. "Who Needs Harvard?" *Atlantic Monthly*, Oct. 2004.

Emling, Shelly. "Retirees Hear a Distant Drum." *International Herald Tribune*, June 25, 2005.

Fenster, Mark. "Community by Covenant: Cohousing and the Contemporary Common Interest Community." *Journal of Land Use & Environmental Law*, 1999.

Free Advice. "Estate Planning—Wills—General Questions." 1995–2007. http://law.freeadvice.com/estate_planning/wills/life_insurance_beneficiaries.htm.

Free Will Docs. "Intestacy—Dying Without a Will." Feb. 5, 2007. http://www.wills-online.com/willsguide/intestacy.asp.

Furnham, Adrian. "The Role of Body Weight, Waist-to-Hip Ratio, and Breast Size in Judgments of Female Attractiveness." *Sex Roles: A Journal of Research*, Aug. 1998.

Gatz, Margaret. "Educating the Brain to Avoid Dementia; Can Mental Exercise Prevent Alzheimer [sic] Disease?" *PLoS Medicine,* Jan. 2005.

Gibson, Lawrence. "Smoking: How Does It Affect Your Skin?" Nov. 15, 2005. Mayo Clinic. http://www.mayoclinic.com/health/smoking/AN00644.

Gillanders, William R. "Long-Term Health Impact of Forced Early Retirement Among Steelworkers." *Journal of Family Practice,* April 1, 1991.

Glassner, Barry. *The Gospel of Food.* New York: HarperCollins, 2007.

Godfrey, David, and David Richardson. "Vitamins and Minerals for Health." *British Food Journal,* vol. 104, no. 11, 2002.

Gonser, Tom. "The RV Industry: Is It Successful?" Nov. 2005. RVers Online. http://www.rversonline.org/EdSuccess.html.

Gordon, Frances. "Top Companies Telecommute." *Dallas Business Journal,* Feb. 17, 2006.

Halligan, Tom. "Alums: Back on Campus." *University Business,* Dec. 2004.

Harris, Jeffrey P. "Dizziness and Benign Positional Vertigo." University of California, San Diego, School of Medicine. http://drviirre.ucsd.edu/Default.aspx?tabid=71.

Higgins, Amy. "Parents, Adult Children Need to Talk Finances." *Cincinnati Enquirer,* July 26, 1998.

Highfield, Roger. "Attractive Women Are More Than Just a Pretty Face." *Telegraph,* Feb. 11, 2005. http://www.telegraph.co.uk/news/main.jhtml?xml=/news/2005/11/02/natt02.xml&sSheet=/portal/2005/11/02/ixportal.html.

Hilton, Lisette. "Straight Talk About Cosmeceuticals." *Dermatology Times,* Jan. 1, 2007.

Holley, Hana. "Retirement Planning Survey Among U.S. Adults Age 40 and Older." AARP (Strategic Issues Research), May 2006. http://www.aarp.org/research/financial/retirementsaving/ret_planning.html.

Homeier, Barbara P. "All About Allergies." June 2005. Kids

Health. http://www.kidshealth.org/parent/medical/allergies/
    allergy.html.
Hong, Peter. "The $200,000 College Diploma." Los Angeles Times,
    Feb. 18, 2007.
"How to Prevent Noise-Induced Hearing Loss." American Family
    Physician, May 1, 2000. http://www.aafp.org/afp/20000501/
    2759ph.html.
"How We Tested Dollar-Store Brands." Consumer Reports.
    http://www.consumerreports.org/cro/health-fitness/drugs
    -supplements/multivitamins-dollarstore-brands-206/index
    .htm.
Hunt, Mary. "Which Bills to Pay First." 2006. Debt-Proof Living.
    http://www.cheapskatemonthly.com/member_back_issue_
    articles.asp?SPID=208&ID=8855.
Ivanhoe Broadcast News. "Cosmetic Surgery Is Now an Option
    for Aging Hands." News 8 Austin, Feb. 24, 2006. http://www
    .news8austin.com/content/living/health_beat/?SecID=169&
    ArID=156199.
Jones, Lisa. "Lifetime of Sex Appeal." Best Life, July–Aug. 2005.
Keegan, Carol, and Sonya Gross. "Boomers at Midlife: The AARP
    Life Stage Study." AARP, 2004. http://www.aarp.org/research/
    reference/boomers/aresearch-import-931.html.
Kim, Jae-Ha. "Raising Eyebrows." Chicago Sun-Times, Aug. 8,
    2000.
Krucoff, Carol. "Insight from Injury." Yoga Journal, May–June
    2003. http://www.healingmoves.com/carol/articles/insight
    .html.
Larson, Aaron. "The Legal Guardianship." Aug. 2003. Expert
    Law. http://www.expertlaw.com/library/estate_planning/
    guardianship.html.
Laux, Marcus, and Christine Conrad. Natural Woman, Natural
    Menopause. New York: HarperCollins, 1997.
Lectric Law Library. "Power of Attorney." 2007. http://www
    .lectlaw.com/filesh/qf104.htm.

Life and Health Insurance Foundation for Education, The. "Life Insurance." 2002. http://www.life-line.org/build/who_needs _it/index.php?pt=lfwni&m=1.

"Long Life, Short Spine." *Deccan Herald*, March 14, 2005. http://www.deccanherald.com/Archives/mar142005/snt9.asp.

Lynch, Brian. "New Allergies Can Hit When Least Expected." April 20, 2006. *Straight*. http://www.straight.com/article/new -allergies-can-hit-when-least-expected.

Macalester College, Psychology Department. "Odor Fatigue." *Smell, the Forgotten Sense*. http://www.macalester.edu/ psychology/whathap/UBNRP/Smell/odor.html.

Mahoney, Sarah. "The Secret Lives of Single Women." *AARP— The Magazine*. May–June 2006.

Markey, Charlotte N. "Understanding Women's Body Satisfaction: The Role of Husbands." *Sex Roles: A Journal of Research*, Aug. 2004.

Matthiessen, Connie. "Age and Fertility: Getting Pregnant in Your 40s." Aug. 2006. Babycenter. http://www.babycenter.com/ refcap/preconception/gettingpregnant/1494699.html.

Mayo Clinic. "Arteriosclerosis/Atherosclerosis." July 1, 2004. http://www.mayoclinic.com/health/arteriosclerosis atherosclerosis/DS00525.

McCamant, Kathryn, and Charles Dirrett. *Cohousing: A Contemporary Approach to Housing Ourselves*. Berkeley, Cal.: Ten Speed Press, 1993.

McCarthy, Alice Buckley. "Who's Having Sex in America?" Sept. 2005. Health Library. http://healthlibrary.epnet.com/ GetContent.aspx?token=dce59228-1023-4705-b1c7 -b407be7b4fc6&chunkiid=14514.

McShane, Larry. "Once Bald Hair Club Now Rides Wave of Success." *Los Angeles Times*, Feb. 4, 1992.

Meadows, Michelle. "Heading Off Hair-Care Disasters: Use Caution with Relaxers and Dyes." *FDA Consumer,* Jan.–Feb. 2001.

"Medical Tests That Can Save Your Life." *Reader's Digest,* Aug. 16, 2005. http://www.rd.com/content/medical-tests-that-can-save -your-life/.

Medline Plus. "Aging Changes in the Senses." July 3, 2004. http:// www.nlm.nih.gov/medlineplus/ency/article/004013.htm.

Melton, Jeffery. "Tummy Tuck vs. Liposuction." http://www .drmelton.com/Chicago/Liposuction/tuck-v-lipo/tuck-v-lipo .html.

MetLife Mature Market Institute and AARP Healthcare Options. "The Future of Retirement Living." June 2004. http://www .metlife.com/WPSAssets/37148187301173737091V1F FutureofRetirementLiving.pdf.

MetLife. "Disability Insurance: An Introduction." 2003–2007. http://www.metlife.com/Applications/Corporate/WPS/CDA/ PageGenerator/0,4132,P1794,00.html.

Meyer, Michelle. "Outsmart Your Midlife Fat Cell." *Better Homes and Gardens,* May 2000.

"Midlife Women Shoulder Burden of Homecare." *A Friend Indeed,* July–August 2003.

Milk, Leslie. "Dying for Color." *Washingtonian,* Aug. 2005.

Molloy, John. *Why Men Marry Some Women and Not Others.* New York: Warner Books, 2003.

Monroe, Valerie. "Beauty Over 40." *O, The Oprah Magazine,* Oct. 2006.

Montenegro, Xenia. "Lifestyles, Dating and Romance: A Study of Midlife Singles." *AARP—The Magazine,* Sept. 2003. http://www .aarp.org/research/family/lifestyles/aresearch-import-522.html.

Mosquera, Gabrielle. "A Safer Way to Dye Hair." *Natural Health,* Aug. 2001.

MotherNature. "Digestive Problems: Calming the Pain and Rumble." http://www.mothernature.com/Library/Bookshelf/ Books/44/23.cfm.

National Family Caregivers Association. "Caregiving Statistics." http://www.thefamilycaregiver.org/who/stats.cfm.

National Institute of Dental and Craniofacial Research. "First-Ever Surgeon General's Report on Oral Health Finds Profound Disparities in Nation's Population." Oct. 5, 2000. http://www.nidcr.nih.gov/NewsandReports/NewsReleases/Archives/NewsRElease05252000.htm.

National Interreligious Service Board for Conscientious Objectors. "Who Is a Conscientious Objector?" Aug. 29, 2006. http://www.scn.org/IP/sdmcc/co.htm.

National Sleep Foundation. "2005 Sleep in America Poll." Mar. 29, 2005. http://www.sleep-solutions.com/phys/education/NSF_2005_Sleep_in_America_Poll_Results.htm.

National Women's Health Resource Center. "National Women's Health Report: Midlife Women & Sexual Health." April 2005. http://www.healthywomen.org/resources/nwhrcpublications/dbpubs/nationalwomenshealthreportmidlifewomensexual healthapril.

Neimark, Jill. "The Beefcaking of America." Psychology Today, Nov.–Dec. 1994.

Nolo. "Bankruptcy." 2007. http://www.nolo.com/resource.cfm/catID/462A9501-9B21-4E09-A08C5A7B8AF51A79/213/161/.

Nolo. "Which Debts Must You Repay?" July 2007. http://www.quickencommunity.com/downloads/docs/making%20and%20Repaying%20Debts.doc.

Nolo. "Wills and Estate Planning." 2007. http://www.nolo.com/resource.cfm/catID/FD1795A9-8049-422C-9087838F86A2BC2B/309/.

Olsen, Deborah Pike. "The Viagra Dialogues." Good Housekeeping, Jan. 2003.

Patterson, Mark T. "Living Wills and Healthcare Power of Attorney." July 2007. FindLaw. http://www.expertlaw.com/library/estate_planning/guardianship.html.

Pedone, Rose-Robin. "Planning to Get Married? Not So Fast." Long Island Business News, Nov. 27, 1998.

Peerce, Donna, and Chuck Cochran. "How to Avoid a Mid-Life Career Crisis." *Career Journal.* http://www.careerjournal.com/myc/fifty/19990323-peerce.html.

Pertschuk, Michael, and Alice Trisdorfer. "Men's Bodies—The Survey." *Psychology Today,* Nov.–Dec. 1993.

Peterson, Jonathan. "Caring Is a Man's Job Too." *Los Angeles Times,* Nov. 27, 2006.

Peterson, Jonathan. "Still on the Job, More Seniors Find Retiring Doesn't Work for Them." *Los Angeles Times,* May 30, 2007.

Phelps, Jerry. "Estrogen Suppression by Compounds Found in Red Wine and Grape Seeds." *Environmental Health Perspectives,* April 2004.

Rae, Stephen. "A Wee Problem." *AARP—The Magazine,* Jan.–Feb. 2005.

Rassman, William R., and Robert M. Bernstein. "Eyebrow Hair Transplants." http://www.bernsteinmedical.com/hair-transplant/eyebrow/index.php.

Roan, Shari. "To Sharpen the Brain, First Hone the Body." *Los Angeles Times,* Jan. 9, 2006.

Rocco, Beatrice. "Revocable Trusts vs. Irrevocable Trusts." Feb. 9, 2007. EZLaw. http://ezarticles.com/?Revocable-Trust(Revocable-Living-Trust)-vs.-Irrevocable-Trusts&id=448578.

Rosenthal, Saul M. *Sex Over 40,* rev. ed. Los Angeles: Tarcher, 2000.

Ross, Kim. "13 Truths About Baby Boomer Travel." 2002. The Association of Travel Marketing Executives. http://www.atme.org/pubs/archives/77_253_1108.cfm.

Rossi, William A. "When Does a Shoe Fit? Nobody Knows." *Footwear News,* March 13, 1995.

Sabo, Eric. "The Other Side of Viagra: Turn Off for Some Women?" *Science Daily,* Sept. 29, 2005. http://sciencedaily.healthology.com/sexual-health/article1204.htm.

Scheinfeld, Noah S. "Getting to the Root of Hair Loss and Its Treatment." *Cortlandt Forum,* Oct. 2005.

Schwartz, Shelly K. "Baby Boomers Are Faced with a Tough Task: Financial Intervention." Nov. 24, 1999. CNN Money. http://money.cnn.com/1999/11/24/life/q_parents/.

Schwartz, Shelly K. "Telecommuting: The Pitch." Sept. 21, 1999. CNN Money. http://money.cnn.com/1999/09/21/life/q_telecommute/.

Shah, J., and N. Christopher. "Can Shoe Size Predict Penile Length?" June 29, 2002. BJU International. http://www.blackwell-synergy.com/doi/pdf/10.1046/j.1464-410X.2002.02974.x?cookieSet=1.

Sherwin, Adam. "Sorry, Girls. The Hunks Are Banned." Times Online, July 27, 2005. http://www.timesonline.co.uk/tol/news/uk/article548439.ece.

SIECUS (Sexuality Information and Education Council of the United States). "Sexuality in Middle and Later Life." http://www.siecus.org/pubs/fact/fact0018.html.

Simmons, Tavia, and Jane Lawler-Dye. "Living with Grandchildren: 2000." Oct. 2003. U.S. Census Bureau. http://www.census.gov/prod/2003pubs/c2kbr-31 pdf

Small, Gary. "What We Need to Know About Age-Related Memory Loss." UCLA Neuropsychiatric Institute. http://www.memory.ucla.edu/home.htm.

Society for Neuroscience. "Smell and the Olfactory System." http://www.sfn.org/index.cfm?pagename=brainBriefings_smellAndTheOlfactorySystem.

Solovitch, Sara. "Let's Get Physical." Los Angeles Times, Feb. 13, 2006.

Somer, Elizabeth. "The Best Vitamins for Women." Prevention, Jan. 2006.

U.S. Department of Health and Human Services. "Medicare." July 12, 2007. http://www.medicare.gov/.

U.S. Department of Labor. "Number of Jobs Held, Labor Market Activity, and Earnings Growth Among Younger Baby Boomers: Recent Results from a Longitudinal Study." Bureau of Labor Statistics News, Aug. 25, 2004.

Ulick, Josh. "Your Daily Allowance." *Newsweek,* Jan. 16, 2006.

Vedder, Richard. "A Fortune in Tuition." *National Review,* Oct. 11, 2004.

Vedder, Richard. *Going Broke by Degree: Why College Costs Too Much.* Washington, D.C.: AEI Press, 2004.

Vestal, Christine. "Retirees Boosting States' Rural Economies." Stateline. http://www.stateline.org/live/ViewPage.action ?siteNodeId=136&languageId=1&contentId=93345.

Washington State Bar Association. "Revocable Living Trusts." Mar. 23, 2006. http://www.wsba.org/media/publications/ pamphlets/revocable.htm.

Waterhouse, Debra. *Outsmarting the Midlife Fat Cell.* New York: Hyperion, 1999.

Weeks, Gerald. "Sex: What problem?" *Psychology Today,* Sept.–Oct. 2002.

Weisman, Robert. "Despite Technology Advances, Office Remains the Place to Be." *Boston Globe,* June 14, 2004.

Weiss, Michael J. "Chasing Youth." *American Demographics,* Oct. 2002.

Wirtz, Ronald A. "Is College Unaffordable?" *Region,* December 2005.

"Workout Woes." Baptist Health. http://www.baptisthealth.net/ bhs/en/health/library/alldetails/0,2585,3150_7232849_ 7396254,00.html

"Wrinkle Creams: Selling Hope in a Jar." *Consumer Reports,* Jan. 2007. http://www.consumerreports.org/cro/health-fitness/ beauty-personal-care/wrinkle-creams-1-07/overview/0107_ cream_ov_1.htm.

INDEX